PHARMACOPEIA

The Most Lamentable Tragedy of William Payne, MD

Gil Kofman

BROADWAY PLAY PUBLISHING INC
224 E 62nd St, NY, NY 10065
www.broadwayplaypub.com
info@broadwayplaypub.com

PHARMACOPEIA
© Copyright 2008 by Gil Kofman

First printing: December 2008
I S B N: 0-88145-425-7

Book design: Marie Donovan
Word processing: Microsoft Word
Typographic controls: Ventura Publisher
Typeface: Palatino
Printed and bound in the U S A

The play premiered in Los Angeles at the Evidence
Room in February 2004. The cast and creative
contributors were:

DOCTOR WILLIAM PAYNE .... Joe Hulser
THERAPIST .... Jessica Morris
RUTH .... Mira Lew
DON FREYBERG .... Matt Kautz
ROGER .... Declan Galvin
T V HOST (DAVE) .... Matt Kautz
MOTHER .... Jessica Morris
YURI .... Deance Wyatt
SENATOR CATES .... Matt Henerson
GOVERNMENT MAN .... Matt Kautz

Director .... Matthew Wilder
Set design .... Efren Delgadillo
Costumes .... Sondra Burns
Lighting .... Brian Lilienthal

CHARACTERS & SETTING

DOCTOR WILLIAM PAYNE, *middle aged man*
THERAPIST, *woman, thirties*
RUTH, DOCTOR PAYNE's *young assistant*
DON FREYBERG, *government F D A, early thirties*
ROGER, *conspiracy nutjob*
T V HOST (DAVE)
MOTHER, *Ms Yankovich, Russian, late thirties*
YURI, *her teenage son*
SENATOR CATES, *fifties*

GOVERNMENT MAN

GOVERNMENT MAN *and* T V HOST *can be played by same actor. Other roles may be double cast as seen fit.*

Time: is Now

Possible Act Break before or after Scene 13

DELUSIONS OF WITTGENSTINIAN GRANDEUR

Scene 1

(DOCTOR WILLIAM PAYNE *appears in the spotlight.*
Addresses the audience.)

DOCTOR PAYNE: Dear Ladies and Gentleman, First off
I want to thank you all for taking the time to come here
tonight to recognize my work. The Nobel Prize is the
elusive dream all great scientists share—and I see a lot
of great scientists in the house tonight. If...*and I say if...*
I don't win the Nobel this evening, it's not because
I don't deserve it, but simply because there are others
here who are just as worthy. But now, now that I'm
here before you all, I just want to say this: ABOUT
FUCKIN TIME!! That's right, about fuckin time I was
recognized. You obsequious buttsucking philistines.
What took you so long?! Don't you know REAL
GENIUS when you see it! *(Suddenly censoring, to himself)*
No. Scratch that. Be more humble. Modest. *Political.*
You can still be considered for other grants. There's
always the MacArthur...a little Guggenheim. *(A deep*
rallying breath before recommencing) Okay okay...
(Another go at it) Ladies and Gentleman, In the
footsteps of Doctor Pasteur...Doctor Watson...and
the incomparable Madame Curie *(twice a Nobel winner)*
let me breathe a sigh of loud satisfaction. If my research
has helped vanquish the terrible dragon, then let that
be my humble and modest gift to such a deserving
humanity. The same way George Washington Carver
(who was black) was obsessed with a...peanut—I (who
incidentally am white) am obsessed with cancer. *(Again*

he quickly corrects himself) No...forget the Black/White thing... Too charged, sensitive. Controversial! *(Resumes his address to audience)* The fact that cancer exists is an insult. *(To himself)* Yes, much better...much. *(Back to audience)* In 1971 President Nixon declared his war against cancer. (Of course he died from a stroke so what would he know.) And today the battle is still going strong with many casualties littering the field. In my book cancer is not only an insult but also a personal affront. A curse that I, personally, am going to remove... an evil I will eventually eradicate. My gauntlet is thrown. The duel between me and the disease is set. *(Stepping to edge of stage)* Any questions? Yes. You in the back. What? Speak up!! My coat...? What about my coat? Why is it... Speak up! I don't understand. What about my coat...? It's covered with blood? *(Pockets of his lab coat fill up with blood.)* Blood? Am I bleeding...? Where? Where am I bleeding? *(He turns pockets inside out. Blood pours out.)*

You call this *blood*? It's not blood. It's it's it's...this is my love for humanity, can't you tell, it just happens to look like blood.

(Lights fade.)

THE NOT-SO SUBTLE AROUSAL OF DOCTOR PAYNE AND THE AFTERMATH OF DESIRE

Scene 2

(Psychiatrist's office. DOCTOR PAYNE *is sitting opposite his* THERAPIST, *he sedulously scrapes his lab coat to remove any last drops of blood.)*

DOCTOR PAYNE: *(Suddenly serious)* So tell me, doc. Seriously. What do you think the blood on the coat is supposed to mean?

THERAPIST: There's no blood on it now.

DOCTOR PAYNE: No. But in the dream I was all covered with it. In my dream, my coat was all covered in blood...

THERAPIST: I'm afraid there's no simple answer.

DOCTOR PAYNE: Why not? WHY NOT?!

THERAPIST: I could offer some kind of conjecture, but most likely it would sound simple and...*reductive.*

DOCTOR PAYNE: Then fuck the blood. Fuck the dream. And let's talk a little more about me.

THERAPIST: That's why we're here.

DOCTOR PAYNE: *(Beat)* You know what I have that others don't even know they lack...?

THERAPIST: I don't....

DOCTOR PAYNE: Confidence!

THERAPIST: Confidence...?

DOCTOR PAYNE: *(Even louder)* CONFIDENCE!! No matter what happens I will not be reduced or discounted. You see, I can think *new thoughts.* Or at least I *think* I do. And that's enough. *That's enough.*

Which is why I never get depressed. I don't just arrange or shift the old thoughts about. I can actually conjure brand new ones from thin air. *(Beat)* That's what gives me confidence to do the kind of work I do.

THERAPIST: And what exactly is your work, Doctor Payne?

(DOCTOR PAYNE stands and drops his pants.)

THERAPIST: What are you doing?

DOCTOR PAYNE: I have a tattoo... on my penis. Explains everything about me and my work.

THERAPIST: Yes, well, perhaps you can just tell me what it says and pull up your pants.

(DOCTOR PAYNE pulls out waistline and peeks inside, reading.)

DOCTOR PAYNE: *"Was mich nicht umbringt..."*

THERAPIST: In German...?

DOCTOR PAYNE: I was drunk at the time. But I liked what it was trying to say.

THERAPIST: *Whatever doesn't kill me...*

DOCTOR PAYNE: Very good. But that's only the first half. You want to read the whole thing I'll need to get an erection.

THERAPIST: Won't be necessary. *(Completes the quote in German.)* *"Was mich nicht umbringt—macht mich stärker."*

DOCTOR PAYNE: That's right. How did you know?

THERAPIST: Nietzcshe.

DOCTOR PAYNE: You're good.

THERAPIST: *(Beat)* You still haven't answered my question.

DOCTOR PAYNE: "That which doesn't kill me, only makes me stronger." *(Beat)* Which goes to say: I'm not a man who normally does this kind of thing.

THERAPIST: *Thing...?*

DOCTOR PAYNE: My lawyer thinks it would look good for the jury. My coming here. Assuming *it* ever goes to trial. Which I highly doubt. But he thinks this would show some effort on my part. This penitence and humility. Kind of like going to confession.

THERAPIST: You might very well surprise yourself...

DOCTOR PAYNE: What's that?

THERAPIST: You might end up liking this kind of...*thing*.

DOCTOR PAYNE: Doubt it. I don't go much for introspection.

THERAPIST: You never know.

DOCTOR PAYNE: I know. And since we're here at *therapy*, I want to start by putting two things on the table: I don't eat vegetables, and I don't suck cock.

THERAPIST: I don't understand what—

DOCTOR PAYNE: Do you masturbate, doctor?

THERAPIST: Excuse me?

DOCTOR PAYNE: Masturbate. How often do you do it?

THERAPIST: I don't see what—

DOCTOR PAYNE: With me it's chronic. I did right before coming here. But the more I do it, the more it needs to be done. You're looking at a man in a perpetual state of soiled virginity. The anticipation, the guilt, the guilt, the anticipation...a vicious cycle where guilt and anticipation become totally interchangeable. Guilt after all is just anticipation in reverse. *(Pause)* Hey, perhaps I should have the tip of my penis stapled like they do

with stomachs these days. Something to curb my
oceanic appetite.

THERAPIST: Have you always been like this?

DOCTOR PAYNE: *(Shocked)* Like what?

THERAPIST: Your first ejaculation. Can you remember it?

DOCTOR PAYNE: They're *all* my *first* ejaculations.
Each and every one of them.

THERAPIST: I see.

DOCTOR PAYNE: And if by chance I miss a day—
wow!—then the entire next day I am obsessed—
simply obsessed—by the fact that I didn't jerk off
the day before and now I feel like I've earned the
right to go full hog—as if I were now treating myself
to some lavish dinner at a four star restaurant.
AMAZING! The *reward* leveraged by just a little
restraint. *(Beat. Wistful.)* But in the end, in the end it's
all one sad fading memory anyway—*what I've done,
ought to have done...* In the end it's all in your head, all
that pain and desire. The consequence of the things
done and not done. *Is my life a dream?* —Philosophers
have asked this for centuries—And when I ejaculate,
does it really matter if this short spurt of happiness was
inspired by some fantasy or spurred on by some fleshy
reality...? What is *BEING* anyway...? And how does
having a penis confuse the issue? *(Turns to her)* Am
I boring you?

THERAPIST: Not at all.

DOCTOR PAYNE: Don't humor me. You think it's all
pretty fuckin pathetic, don't you?

THERAPIST: No.

DOCTOR PAYNE: All this attention focused on my
flaccid tattooed penis?

THERAPIST: Not necessarily.

DOCTOR PAYNE: I can see by your face. You think it's idiotically indulgent.

THERAPIST: On the contrary. It might prove—

DOCTOR PAYNE: Then why do you keep looking at your watch.

THERAPIST: I wasn't—

DOCTOR PAYNE: Yeah, yeah, yeah. Checking your watch every five seconds, even though you charge using a forty-five minute hour.

THERAPIST: I'm sorry.

DOCTOR PAYNE: Maybe I should actually *dramatize* one of these so-called solitary outings for you in greater detail...paint a better picture of my *solipsistic* love life...the so-called "celebration of the self" that is me...?

THERAPIST: If you think it would be helpful, go ahead.

DOCTOR PAYNE: Alright. Fasten your seatbelt, because here it is: THE AROUSAL OF DOCTOR PAYNE AND THE AFTERMATH OF DESIRE. *(He gets up, goes to window.)* May I...?

(THERAPIST *nods approvingly and* DOCTOR PAYNE *twists open the Venetian blinds. Afternoon light lances into the room. Throwing exaggerated shadows all around)*

DOCTOR PAYNE: Usually I'll initiate the ritual at sunset, not because of any romantic bullshit, I mean it's pretty hard to get romantic over yourself, but because that's when the sun rakes low into my bedroom and casts this long glorious shadow of my erect phallus against the far wall... *(He grows visibly aroused.)* ...my erect penis now magnified *ten times* its original size and projected on the wall like some giant movie screen. So veined and muscular—

THERAPIST: *(Cutting him off)* Oh, I'm so sorry, Doc. But I'm afraid our time is up.

DOCTOR PAYNE: You haven't even checked your watch.

THERAPIST: *(Checks it)* We can continue next time.

DOCTOR PAYNE: But...but...I've just started. I can't stop before I've even started.

THERAPIST: Next time.

DOCTOR PAYNE: *(Coitus interruptus)* I don't want to wait for next time.

THERAPIST: I'm sorry, but I've got another patient waiting.

(THERAPIST opens door for DOCTOR PAYNE to leave.)

DOCTOR PAYNE: One last question. Where's the bathroom? *(He untucks his shirt to cover his erection before standing.)*

(Lights fade.)

EVERY SELF-PROCLAIMED GENIUS NEEDS A GOOD DOSE OF REASSURANCE AND LOVE

Scene 3

(Doctor's office. Reception area)

DON: Are you sure he's not in.

RUTH: I'm sorry but you should've made an appointment. Doctor is very busy.

DON: I tried, but no one would take my call.

RUTH: Are you sure you called the right number?

DON: Are you, Ruth?

RUTH: Yes, I am.

DON: You have a lovely voice, Ruth.

RUTH: Thank you.

DON: I'm Mister Freyburg. Don Freyburg with the—

RUTH: I know who you are.

DON: I believe we spoke on the phone before.

RUTH: Did we...?

DON: Yes. I'm the person who keeps calling, asking to see Doctor Payne. And you're the one who keeps plying me with all kinds of excuses as to why he's not available at this particular point in time.

RUTH: Are you sure it was me.

DON: *(Smiles, glib)* No. Maybe I'm mistaken. Yes, now that you call my attention to it, I'm sure it's my own *wrongheadedness* that's led me astray here. After all, how could someone with all your extravagant charms be such a flagrant liar.

RUTH: At least you find me charming.

(Phone rings. RUTH answers.)

RUTH: *(Into phone)* Yes, doctor. No. There's a certain Dan Freyburg here to see you.

DON: *(Correcting her)* Don. *Don* Freyburg.

RUTH: What...? No. No appointment. I see. Yes. I'll make sure to tell him. Bye. *(She hangs up. Smiles widely, disingenuously)* The doctor will be glad to make your acquaintance, but he seems to be stuck in traffic.

DON: Why doesn't that surprise me?

RUTH: You should've made an—

DON: Appointment. Yes yes. *(Beat)* Does he know who I am?

RUTH: The doctor is informed.

(DON prepares to leave.)

RUTH: You going...?

DON: Sound disappointed.

RUTH: I was thinking of the doctor. He'll be very sorry to have missed you.

DON: *(Flirtatiously)* What about you...? Are you sorry to see me go?

RUTH: Only if you promise never to come back.

DON: Oh, I'll be back. You can count on that. Tell the doctor I'm gonna make my *own* appointment. The government doesn't take too kindly to this kind of shoddy evasion.

(DON leaves. DOCTOR PAYNE enters from inner office with cell phone in hand.)

DOCTOR PAYNE: Very determined young man. Not half-bad looking too.

RUTH: I think you should meet with them, doctor. For your own good.

DOCTOR PAYNE: You seemed to be enjoying yourself.

RUTH: I was trying to get rid of him.

DOCTOR PAYNE: *(Touch of jealousy)* I know. I heard. Must be nice to be flattered by young man like that.

RUTH: I was waiting for you to call, doctor.

DOCTOR PAYNE: *(Mocking RUTH)* "The doctor will be very sorry to have missed you."

RUTH: Please Doc.

DOCTOR PAYNE: "You have a lovely voice, Ruth."

RUTH: Don't do this.

DOCTOR PAYNE: What about you...? How sorry were you to see *him* go?

RUTH: You should've called sooner if you wanted him to leave earlier.

DOCTOR PAYNE: My phone needed recharging. That's the trouble with these fuckin cell phones...aside from giving you fuckin brain cancer, they always need to be fuckin recharged. Fuck! *(Beat)* You like me Ruth?

RUTH: How could I not, doctor? After what you've done for me...my family.

DOCTOR PAYNE: But do you think I'm a *good* man?

RUTH: You know I do. You are different doctor. I understand you.

DOCTOR PAYNE: Do you?

RUTH: It must've been very painful for you when your wife died.

DOCTOR PAYNE: Unspeakable. She kept thinking I could save her, but there was nothing I could do. Nothing.

RUTH: I'm so sorry.

(DOCTOR PAYNE pulls a blonde wig out from a drawer and smells it.)

DOCTOR PAYNE: Today I try to preserve her memory in my work. As if saving others might bring her back.

RUTH: That's why I like working for you doctor. Your empathy is... boundless.

DOCTOR PAYNE: But what about my work, Ruth? Forget *me* for a moment. Do you believe in my work?

RUTH: You know I do doctor.

DOCTOR PAYNE: Tell me again. When the whole world is against you, a little *more* praise can't hurt.

RUTH: You are a genius doctor. Like you often said yourself: "I may be an asshole, but I'm also a genius"

DOCTOR PAYNE: Yes. Yes I am.

RUTH: And I want to spend the rest of my life ministering to all your *unsatisfied* needs. *(She drops to her knees.)* Day and night, I want to pleasure the monumental obelisk of your tattooed manhood.

DOCTOR PAYNE: Are you sure you wouldn't prefer that nice young man who stopped by earlier.

RUTH: Never Doctor. Never. You're the only one I care about.

(RUTH unzips DOCTOR PAYNE's pants.)

DOCTOR PAYNE: You know how much I like when you talk this way, Ruth. How I admire the passion behind your words. But I'm not sure we have time to go through the whole scenario right now.

RUTH: Next appointment is not for another hour, doctor.

DOCTOR PAYNE: Alright. Here.

(DOCTOR PAYNE offers RUTH his dead wife's blonde wig.)

RUTH: *(Whining)* I'd rather wear the surgical mask.

DOCTOR PAYNE: Please.

RUTH: But it gets so hot under this.

DOCTOR PAYNE: You know how much it means to me. *(He inhales the wig.)* This is how I remember her before she lost her hair.

RUTH: *(Relenting)* And I'm here to help you forget. I am the antidote, doctor. I am the antidote.

DOCTOR PAYNE: *(In a transport)* My poor beloved Angeline. The way her hair smelled just after it was washed, or how it bounced in the warm afternoon light. Never did a wife love her husband more, or a husband care so much for his wife. The months I spend ministering to her every need...changing the sheets,

taking her temperature, emptying the bedpan, refilling
the feeding tube....

(DOCTOR PAYNE *places the wig on her head. Turning on a
dime, the submissive* RUTH *takes charge. Shrill, aggressive
and matrimonial—she adopts the dead wife's persona.*)

RUTH: WAIT! Wait a minute. Before I lie down or do
anything else here, I need to know if you changed the
roll of paper on this table like I asked you to?

DOCTOR PAYNE: Yes, honey.

RUTH: What about the heat? Don't you think you
should turn up the heat.

DOCTOR PAYNE: Yes, dear.

RUTH: You should also get a haircut. So you look more
respectable for your patients.

DOCTOR PAYNE: Whatever you say, dear.

RUTH: I know *I* don't count—why should I? But let me
tell you, no one wants Gene Wilder for their doctor.

DOCTOR PAYNE: Maybe you should lie down, honey.

RUTH: Don't rush me. Would you rush your wife?
Would you?!

DOCTOR PAYNE: No.

RUTH: I hate when you rush me.

DOCTOR PAYNE: Sorry, sweetums.

RUTH: I'll let you know when I'm ready.

DOCTOR PAYNE: Of course, dear. Of course.

RUTH: Now my head hurts, see what you've done?!
If only you took better care of me...

DOCTOR PAYNE: I'm sorry.

RUTH: Some Doctor you are. I can feel a migraine the
size of Hiroshima coming on.

DOCTOR PAYNE: If there's anything I can do—

RUTH: It's too late for that, you quack. No wonder I got cancer. No wonder! *(She tears off wig.)*

DOCTOR PAYNE: *(Losing it entirely)* Put that wig back on you bitch! For fifteen years you kvetch nonstop and then you just die. I'll tell you when you can die. Now lie down and shut up! *(He unzips his trousers and prepares to mount her.)*

(Lights fade)

THE KARMIC KISS OF X-RAYS

Scene 4

(DOCTOR PAYNE's office. Clean and polished, fairly high tech, hard to tell where the walls end and the modern art covering them begins.)

(DOCTOR PAYNE is consulting with a young MOTHER, Mrs Yankovich, and her son, YURI.)

MOTHER: *(Apologetic)* I was here at two-thirty but you were busy —

DOCTOR PAYNE: Don't worry about it, you're catching me at my best right now. *(He zips up fly.)* My mind is always clearest in the afternoon...after a little physical exercise. Do you exercise? You look like a woman with good circulation?

MOTHER: Thank you, doctor.

DOCTOR PAYNE: Let me listen to your pulse.

MOTHER: Actually I'm here with my son.

DOCTOR PAYNE: Your son?!

MOTHER: Yuri.

(YURI *crawls out from under the table.*)

DOCTOR PAYNE: *This* is yours?! *(Turns away, overlap)*
I take it you've seen other doctors.

MOTHER: Well—

DOCTOR PAYNE: *(Cutting her off)* And I'm your last
resort.

MOTHER: We did try some more conventional methods
first.

DOCTOR PAYNE: *(Aggrieved)* And now you come here.
To me. After everything else fails you come here...
to the office of Doctor Payne.

MOTHER: Please...

DOCTOR PAYNE: You think I like being an alternate...
your last choice in a list of choices? But no matter.
No point in taking things personally. Especially when
you're the best.

MOTHER: We need your help, Doctor.

DOCTOR PAYNE: Before we start, one thing we should
be absolutely clear about is— No Guarantees. Whoever
tells you otherwise, is lying. *(To YURI)* Remove your
shirt.

(YURI *does.* DOCTOR PAYNE *listens to his chest, talks.*)

DOCTOR PAYNE: Contrary to common opinion, a
doctor's job isn't to prevent death. No one can do that.
Except god, but maybe that's why we invented him.
(Beat) Please cough.

(YURI *obliges.*)

DOCTOR PAYNE: Now as farfetched as this may seem
to you, we are working together here. In concert. To
banish this dread disease from your body. I may be the
doctor, but you...

(DOCTOR PAYNE *looks through charts,* MOTHER *fills in.*)

MOTHER: ...Yuri.

DOCTOR PAYNE: Yes, you Yuri, you play a bigger role—you are "the patient". And together we are accomplices. Understand...? We are a team!

(DOCTOR PAYNE *lifts up hand for a high five.* YURI *doesn't respond.*)

MOTHER: Yuri. The doctor asked you something.

DOCTOR PAYNE: High five

MOTHER: Yuri

DOCTOR PAYNE: Low five.

MOTHER: YURI*!*

DOCTOR PAYNE: A team...

(YURI *weakly gives* DOCTOR PAYNE *a high five slap, but* DOCTOR PAYNE *pulls away.*)

DOCTOR PAYNE: Too slow. Now first thing I need to know is do you want to be cured? Sounds so simple it's almost silly. But not really, not everyone wants to be cured. Sure the disease can be painful, death itself frightening, but why does one contract the disease in the first place? Asbestos? Something you ate? Electrical power lines encasing your home and school? Or could it simply be hereditary? A time bomb lurking in the *portfolio* of your genes, ready to ambush you at the least convenient moment. (*Pause*) Or maybe it's just weakness of will, lack of resolve? Karma...? Bad ugly karma that throws its long dark shadow from one unhappy life to the next. (*He prepares to draw blood from* YURI.) Now this might pinch a bit. So I suggest you look at that lovely painting on the wall—

YURI: Which one?

DOCTOR PAYNE: Doesn't matter. It's modern art.

YURI: But—

MOTHER: Don't argue with the Doctor honey.

(DOCTOR PAYNE inspects the needle, tapping it.)

DOCTOR PAYNE: I see you prefer to close your eyes?

YURI: I wasn't sure what I was supposed to see.

DOCTOR PAYNE: So you decided to shut your eyes?

YURI: I'm sorry, I...

DOCTOR PAYNE: There's nothing to be scared of, Yuri. After all, it's the *not-knowing* that brings us all together. *(He draws blood. It leaks on his coat.)* SHIT! Shit!

MOTHER: Something wrong Doctor?

DOCTOR PAYNE: My coat. Yuri's blood. I just had it cleaned!

MOTHER: We're so sorry. *(Admonishing to her son)* Yuri, apologize to the doctor.

YURI: But I—

MOTHER: Apologize. NOW!

YURI: I'm sorry, Doctor.

DOCTOR PAYNE: That's okay. It's okay. If you step into the next room my nurse will take some x-rays. Ruth!!

MOTHER: Go on, son. Go.

(RUTH enters and leads YURI away. DOCTOR PAYNE alone with MOTHER. He reads the boy's chart before looking up. Then tosses a coin)

DOCTOR PAYNE: The prognosis isn't very bright. But then again you wouldn't be here if you didn't already know that. *(Catches coin)* Heads or tails?

MOTHER: Please, is there anything we can do, doctor.

DOCTOR PAYNE: *Medulloblastomas* is a very predictable and pernicious cancer. *(Looks at coin)* Heads! *(Tosses again)* Predictable precisely because it's so pernicious.

MOTHER: We'll do anything. Anything at all.

DOCTOR PAYNE: My treatment you understand is highly unorthodox.

MOTHER: I don't care.

DOCTOR PAYNE: Some would even say...*unethical.* *(Catches coin)* Heads or tails?

MOTHER: I don't know.

DOCTOR PAYNE: Guess.

MOTHER: But I don't want to guess.

DOCTOR PAYNE: It's all random anyway. Each toss a new start. A fresh beginning. *(With relish) Tabula rasa.*

*(*MOTHER *still hesitates, shakes her head "no".)*

DOCTOR PAYNE: Okay...how about you guess— but I won't look.

MOTHER: Then how will you—

DOCTOR PAYNE: Heads or tails?

MOTHER: Tails.

DOCTOR PAYNE: Why not Heads?

MOTHER: You said it didn't matter.

DOCTOR PAYNE: It doesn't. Important thing is you made a choice. *(Pockets coin)* With me, you'll be trespassing into a new frontier of medicine...are you sure you're ready for that? All that risk and uncertainty... You don't seem like the gambling type.

MOTHER: I'm here.

*(*DOCTOR PAYNE *offers* MOTHER *a seat.)*

DOCTOR PAYNE: Sit down.

(MOTHER *remains standing.)*

MOTHER: I'd pull all my hair out, doctor, and run naked in the middle of traffic if I thought it might save my son.

DOCTOR PAYNE: Shhh...there's no need to talk this way. But you should be aware that there is a very long waiting list before I can admit any new patients...

MOTHER: Please help me.

DOCTOR PAYNE: You're very eloquent in your suffering and pain, Ms Yankovich. But some of the drugs are very hard to come by.

MOTHER: Please. *(She gets on her knees.)*

DOCTOR PAYNE: Very expensive *and* experimental.

MOTHER: If you want me to beg, I will.

DOCTOR PAYNE: I'm not saying your suffering is not genuine. How can it not be...? But you have to be realistic here.

MOTHER: I pray every night for my son.

DOCTOR PAYNE: I'm sure you do.

MOTHER: Every night I pray with all my heart thinking how can God not hear me when I'm praying so deeply.

DOCTOR PAYNE: *(Beat)* Have I already told you that you hold a remarkable resemblance to my wife...?

MOTHER: You married?

DOCTOR PAYNE: Widowed.

MOTHER: Then you must know how I feel.

DOCTOR PAYNE: Perhaps there's a way we can make this work. Yes, I'm sure we can do something. Now go join your son for an x-ray and let me see what I can work out here.

MOTHER: But I'm not sick...

DOCTOR PAYNE: Go on. Humor me. X-rays don't hurt.
I want to ascertain the goodness of your heart. And
X-rays can penetrate all the way inside, like some soft
whispered word, but for some strange reason you can't
feel them. No matter how deep they go, you cannot feel
them. But it would make me so happy.

(Lights fade)

DOCTOR PAYNE'S TELEGENIC PHILOSOPHY REPUDIATES THE PURITAN IDEAL AND WELCOMES THE NAKED TRUTH

Scene 5

(T V Station. The HOST, *Dave, looks anxiously about for
his guest.*

HOST: Tonight, joining us live from Las Vegas, where
his clinic is on the front lines of the deadly war against
cancer—as well as caught in the scrutinizing crosshairs
of the F D A—is Doctor William Payne, one of the
leading and most controversial doctors leading this
uphill battle against this dread disease.

(No DOCTOR PAYNE*)*

HOST: *(Forced to improvise)* A doctor...who has his hands
full not only with cancer, but also with a government
that scrutinizes and regulates his every move.... This a
free country or is another Waco brewing in the halls of
the F D A? After this!

*(*DOCTOR PAYNE *stumbles in—as they finally go to
commercial break.)*

DOCTOR PAYNE: *(Cinching his belt)* Are we on?

HOST: Just went to commercial. Where were you?

DOCTOR PAYNE: Where do I sit?

HOST: You missed your entrance.

DOCTOR PAYNE: I was busy in the bathroom.

HOST: We had to open without you.

DOCTOR PAYNE: Well, I'm here now. And lucky for you, you're catching me at my best right now. *(He zips up.)*

HOST: Nervous?

DOCTOR PAYNE: About what?

HOST: No one could find you.

DOCTOR PAYNE: I told you. I was in the men's room. *(Beat)* By the way your *intern* seems *verrry* talented...

HOST: *(Tentative, betrayed)* Cathy...?!

DOCTOR PAYNE: Is that her name? Very smart, quick. Good sense of humor too.

HOST: We only hire ivy leaguers at this station.

DOCTOR PAYNE: Really? Well, in that case, rather than referring to her as a nice piece of ass, let me be so bold as to say she's equipped with an *exquisite derriere.*

HOST: Of course some of these D-gals have a chip on their shoulder—this being cable, not network—but the work is *first* rate. Our show is extremely popular. Terrific ratings. *(Beat)* This your first time on television?

DOCTOR PAYNE: In this kind of format, yes. Most of my patients I meet through internet...or word of mouth.

HOST: You'll have millions of listeners here. We're simultaneously broadcast on radio as well as T V.

DOCTOR PAYNE: *(Sarcastic)* Maybe I should speak louder then?

HOST: No need for that, Doc. Just make sure to look at the camera with the red light. Ready...?

DOCTOR PAYNE: Since the day I was born.

HOST: *(Happy for the distraction)* Ok. We're back.
And joining us today is the hot and controversial
Doctor Payne. The man who may just save your life
with what you flush away. *(Turning to* DOCTOR PAYNE*)*
Doctor Payne is it true that America is lagging in its
search for a cancer cure?

DOCTOR PAYNE: You're asking a very important
question, Dave.

HOST: Thank you.

DOCTOR PAYNE: *(Overriding)* Which I think leads us
to dwell on an even deeper one—which is: *Why?*

HOST: Why...?

DOCTOR PAYNE: *Why cure cancer in the first place?*
Is that what we, as a country, really want?

HOST: Surely you must be joking, doctor.

DOCTOR PAYNE: Cancer is no joke, Dave. Face the facts.
We spend a mere two billion dollars a year on cancer
research versus fourteen billion a year on pornography?
What does that tell you... right there? What...?

*(*HOST *shrugs.)*

DOCTOR PAYNE: Exactly. Now I'm the last person
on earth to object to a *good pornographic-night-out-
on-the-town...* But the question I must ask myself is—
Am I simply curing the sick so they can jerk off more
diligently once they are restored to normal health?
Is that our priority here...the true purpose of my job?

HOST: Don't you think you're mixing apples and
oranges, Doc?

DOCTOR PAYNE: Not at all. Because in spite of the tacit
acceptance of pornography in this country, America
is still a very Puritanical place. People here believe in

repentance and redemption as a means of purification. As if the only way to get healthy or have a second chance were to undergo a certain dose of *cleansing* through some corrosive chemo and radiation.

HOST: And your regime, doctor, how does it differ from what's out there now?

DOCTOR PAYNE: To start with, I believe the body is a self-sustained system that manufactures all it needs. Rather than *punish* it back to health, we simply have to find a way to tap into our body's unique chemistry to arrive at the proper cure.

HOST: Would you then say your methods are more innovative or experimental than what's out there now?

DOCTOR PAYNE: Let's get one thing straight. For me there is no such thing as *experimental*. Until we have a working cure, all treatments—conventional and alternative—are experimental.

HOST: I'm sure the F D A would beg to disagree.

DOCTOR PAYNE: Screw the F D A. I'm kosher as the next guy, Dave.

HOST: No one's arguing your legitimacy, Doc. But wouldn't you say that drinking piss is somewhat out of the ordinary, even if it is kosher piss. *(He gives a self-satisfied chuckle.)*

DOCTOR PAYNE: What I give my patients, *with their consent of course*, is a suspension of neoplastin peptides in water.

HOST: *Peptides...?*

DOCTOR PAYNE: Peptides are a protein based substance produced by the body.

HOST: *(Overriding)* Which, if I'm not mistaken, is normally found in... urine.

DOCTOR PAYNE: We are currently in the process of extracting the peptides through an entirely synthetic means.

HOST: But in the meantime people are actually drinking piss, am I right?

DOCTOR PAYNE: One must look at the results of a cure not the origin. I mean who cares that penicillin came from some sickening mold on a piece of bread? The question is how can it help us. *(Beat)* You mind if I get a little intimate here, Dave.

HOST: Perhaps it's time we check the phone lines now... Seems like we have a very urgent caller on Line 1. Hello. You're on the air.

CALLER: *(V O)* Hi! I'm calling from the hospital where they tell me I'm dying...

HOST: Sorry but you'll have to speak up. We can't hear you.

CALLER: *(V O)* I'm calling from my cell phone. At the hospital.

HOST: I see. That explains the poor connection.

CALLER: *(V O)* They're giving me chemo now. As we speak.

HOST: Which hospital is that?

CALLER: *(V O)* Fuck. It's killing me. *(He throws up on other end of line. Then dry heaves.)* I don't know how much longer I can take it. I need to talk to the doctor. *(Vomits again.)* I need to know if he's ever helped someone with stage 3 glioma...

(CALLER vomits once more and line goes dead.)

HOST: Ooo. I think we lost him on that one, doc. Stage 3... that's pretty serious isn't it. Even for a miracle worker like you, I mean....

DOCTOR PAYNE: *(Overlap)* Tell me, Dave, have you ever lost anyone to cancer?

HOST: My mother.

DOCTOR PAYNE: When was that?

HOST: Last year.

DOCTOR PAYNE: I'm sorry. What was her name?

HOST: Louise.

DOCTOR PAYNE: Beautiful name. Louise. Beautiful. *(Beat)* Do you miss her?

HOST: Every minute.

DOCTOR PAYNE: If Louise were *my* patient, Dave, I can assure you she'd still be here. Louise might have had to imbibe a little...*urine* as you so aptly pointed out before, but right now she'd be sitting where I'm sitting. With us. You.

HOST: Folks at home may remember how she always asked to come on the show. But I always said *no*. Thought it might be inappropriate. Unprofessional. *(He starts sobbing, blows into Kleenex.)*

DOCTOR PAYNE: We've all suffered loss, Dave. All of us have suffered. And that's why we must look beyond the suffering...to life. To happiness. By the way, your intern...

HOST: Cathy...?

DOCTOR PAYNE: She wants you to come over right after the show and pick up your stuff.

(Lights fade)

DOCTOR PAYNE OFFERS THE ELIXIR OF LIFE IN THE CUP OF CHILDHOOD.

Scene 6

(DOCTOR PAYNE's office. He stands in the corner peeing desperately into a child's Disney thermos.)

DOCTOR PAYNE: Did you find them Ruth?

RUTH: (O S) On your table, Doctor.

DOCTOR PAYNE: What would I do without you.

(DOCTOR PAYNE recaps thermos and crosses to table. Removes a set of X-rays from a large envelope. Slides them into several lightboxes. And is soon surrounded by the monochromatic glow of X-rays mounted in lightboxes.)

(DOCTOR PAYNE lies on table, begins to masturbate.)

DOCTOR PAYNE: (Russian accent) Ah Miss Yankovich, you might've taken off your shirt for me, but this... this... is what I'm really interested in. The real you without the clothes, without your little boy, under the skin, beneath the bones...

(Intercom Buzzes. DOCTOR PAYNE drops the accent.)

DOCTOR PAYNE: What is it?! I told you I don't want to be disturbed. I'm in the middle of a sensitive procedure.

RUTH: (O S/Intercom) I'm sorry, Doctor. But I thought you might want to know you took her son's X-rays by mistake.

DOCTOR PAYNE: Fuck! No wonder it was taking so long.

RUTH: I've got the mother's set out here if you want to switch them.

DOCTOR PAYNE: Quick, quick. Slide the new ones under the door, will you? And hurry!

(RUTH *does.* DOCTOR PAYNE *pops them in the light box. Begins to beat off again.*)

DOCTOR PAYNE: *(Russian accent)* Oh yeah. Oh yeah!! Now that's better Ms Yankovich. Much better.

(Another buzzer)

DOCTOR PAYNE: Just a minute. Just a goddamn minute!

RUTH: *(O S)* I'm sorry, Doctor, but—

DOCTOR PAYNE: I'll be right there. *(He reaches for Kleenex.)*

RUTH: *(O S)* It's Senator Cates, doctor.

DOCTOR PAYNE: I'm on my way.

(DOCTOR PAYNE *opens door. Greets* SENATOR CATES *with a hearty handshake, while still wiping his hands.*)

DOCTOR PAYNE: Well, well, well, Senator Cates. To what do I owe this great honor?

SENATOR CATES: I'm dying, doctor.

DOCTOR PAYNE: Cancer?

SENATOR CATES: Astrocytoma.

DOCTOR PAYNE: Now that you mention it you don't look so good. Please sit down.

SENATOR CATES: I hope I'm not catching you at a bad time.

DOCTOR PAYNE: Actually you're catching me at my best. *(He smiles, switches off the fluorescent box with x-rays. And zips up.)* I may be wrong, but didn't you testify against me at the government deposition two years ago?

SENATOR CATES: Yes I did.

DOCTOR PAYNE: And now you're here. Isn't life a piece of work. You must be very desperate. To come here. Like this.

SENATOR CATES: I saw you on television.

DOCTOR PAYNE: Did you...?

SENATOR CATES: Your voice sounded so reassuring... what you said... I...

DOCTOR PAYNE: You figured you had nothing to lose.

SENATOR CATES: *(Overlapping)* It held such promise. *(Pause)* You have to help me doctor. Soon as I saw you on tv, heard your voice I knew I had to come here. But you mustn't tell a soul or I'll shut you the fuck down. Understand...? This is strictly confidential.

DOCTOR PAYNE: Always is.

SENATOR CATES: I'm still good for another term here. I need you to help me.

DOCTOR PAYNE: If I can, I will.

SENATOR CATES: Cure me, son, and you'll never have to worry about research grant money again. I can swing that vote you need for approval. F D A will never trouble you again. And all you gotta do is cure me.

DOCTOR PAYNE: And if I can't.

SENATOR CATES: You have to.

DOCTOR PAYNE: I'll try. But even if god himself walked through that door with cancer I'd say: Sorry, pal, no guarantees, not today. You can have your covenants and vows and sacrifices galore, but if you want guarantees go to the government. They're good at bonding their lies. *(He produces the Disney thermos he pissed in earlier, and pours urine into its cup.)* Drink this.

SENATOR CATES: What is it? Smells like asparagus.

DOCTOR PAYNE: Peptides suspended in a water solution. Drink.

SENATOR CATES: I asked you what it is. Not a recitation of the periodic table.

DOCTOR PAYNE: Urine.

SENATOR CATES: You're shitting me.

DOCTOR PAYNE: *My* urine.

SENATOR CATES: I don't care whose urine it is. You think Senator Cates the III is going to drink piss, you've got another thing coming.

DOCTOR PAYNE: Other patients, I give them urine from the urinal. You...you I make an exception. I pee for you myself. V I P urine. *Very Important Piss*. Now drink! This derivative will reverse, if not fully resolve, the growth of your tumor. *(Long pause)* You want to live?

(SENATOR CATES *still hesitates.*)

SENATOR CATES: I...I...can't.

DOCTOR PAYNE: Then there's nothing I can do to help you. Goodbye Senator. *(He opens door.)*

SENATOR CATES: But—

DOCTOR PAYNE: When I first came to America twenty years ago I made Disneyland my first stop. That's where I got this lovely thermos. Anyway, soon as I got off the plane I took a cab to Mickey's magic kingdom. Because to understand the adult, one has to first understand the child in the adult. But what I saw there was more terrifying than anything I could imagine. Here at Disneyland the adult *was* the child. There was no difference. Everywhere you looked. There were more adults than children. Adults who had never really bothered to grow up. Adults who thought that by diverting themselves at Disneyland they might remain kids forever and avoid death altogether...

SENATOR CATES: Just get to the damn point. I'm dying here.

DOCTOR PAYNE: Point is that children must often be forced to take their medicine if they're to get better, Senator. And in America the child is not much different from the adult. That's my point, Senator. So with all due respect... DRINK THE FUCK UP!

SENATOR CATES: I am not a child.

DOCTOR PAYNE: Really? Your cars, money, family, home. They'll all be orphaned without you. Drink!

SENATOR CATES: I...

(Holds out the Disney cup to him.)

DOCTOR PAYNE: Drink!

(SENATOR CATES lifts it to his mouth but stops.)

SENATOR CATES: I...

DOCTOR PAYNE: You came here because you thought I could help you.

SENATOR CATES: Yes.

DOCTOR PAYNE: You were the one who called the T V station, weren't you?

SENATOR CATES: How did you know...?

DOCTOR PAYNE: You called from the chemo ward, didn't you?

SENATOR CATES: I...

DOCTOR PAYNE: It was you. Begging for my help. Vomiting over the air. I can always tell a person by the sound of their vomit. It was you with Stage 3 glioma. Calling and vomiting all over the air like that.

SENATOR CATES: Yes.

DOCTOR PAYNE: Then do what I say.

SENATOR CATES: Now look you--—

DOCTOR PAYNE: What's a little urine amongst the living.

SENATOR CATES: I-

DOCTOR PAYNE: Drink.

SENATOR CATES: You got a straw?

(DOCTOR PAYNE *smiles.*)

DOCTOR PAYNE: I'll be right back.

(SENATOR CATES *steels himself. Lifts up Disney cup.
As he begins to drink...*)

(*Lights fade.*)

GOD WORKS IN MYSTERIOUS WAYS AND IN PLACES YOU'D NEVER THINK TWICE OF...

Scene 7

(*Casino. Men's restroom.* DOCTOR PAYNE *goes from urinal
to urinal collecting piss with a giant syringe. Then injecting
it into his thermos.*)

(*Against the wall is a line of toilet stalls. One of them is
occupied by a man,* ROGER, *busy evacuating himself,
grunting obscenely.*)

ROGER: For forty days and fifty nights I'm wandering
lost through the desert eating nothing but cactus
and scorpions and drinking my own piss, if you can
actually believe that. Then on the fortieth day, with
Death Valley at my back, I finally see it before me,
the bejeweled city of light. (*He grunts.*) You like Vegas?
I love it! LOVE IT! You ask me I think Vegas is the
holiest place on earth, more than Mecca or the Wailing
Wall, here in Vegas you can hear the chatter of people
praying non-stop, day and night, just to get another

good hand.

Anyway, just so happens that the day I got to Vegas was the day Roy Horn was mauled by his favorite white tiger while Siegfried was doing god knows what backstage. I remember being in the audience that night, and let me tell you it was NO accident. No sirree! Did you know that in the old days the lion tamer used to calm the beasts by jerking them off right before the show. Well, let me tell you, old Montcore the tiger wasn't in the best mood the night I saw him, and I wouldn't be surprised if Siegfried or Roy neglected their duties that day.

Anyway that night, while Roy is racing down the strip in an ambulance, I went for a long stroll trying to make sense of things. Virtually I walked the whole globe in a matter of minutes, like I was god himself, past the Eiffel tower, the Sphinx, a few paddles on a gondola at the Venetian, and then the Statue of Liberty; I traversed countries and telescoped continents with almost every step I took, as if my luck could change with each new venue. And then it came to me. I heard the Blue Men speaking to me in god's secret tongue. *(He makes gibberish noises)* God wanted me to replace Roy in the act. *Siegfried And Roy* was now going to be *Siegfried And Roger*. Or better yet, *Roger And Siegfried*. That's my name, Roger. But when Roy survived the attack and Siegfried kicked me out of his green room, I knew my destiny lay somewhere else. So I left the Mirage and went to the Stardust where Wayne Newton was singing *Danke Schoen*. Because any guy who can sing like that and not be totally gay deserves some kind of support and recognition. So I strut into the casino feeling like a million bucks because something inside tells me that's what I'm gonna win that night—a million bucks! Trouble is I'm penniless, more broke than M C Hammer, when I hear a payphone ringing on the street, so of course I answer it but it's the wrong number.

Although when I hang up a quarter drops (ding!)
like a message from God on my answering machine—
and I know I can either use this quarter to call my
mother, or I can drop it in a slot machine and see what
happens.
  Well pretty soon one thing leads to another and this
quarter turns into a bucket full of change. And next
thing you know I'm at the blackjack table, then the
roulette table. And pretty soon that one stray quarter
becomes three hundred thousand dollars. Wow! Talk
about magic! You have any idea how much explosives
three hundred thousand dollars will buy? I'm talking
the local garden variety type made with fertilizer. 9/11
thing only cost five hundred thousand. So anyway I'm
at the crap table now and I'm amassing a fucking
fortune. I can't lose, no matter how hard I try I can't
even come close. Because, like I said, this here is all
God's work. And me winning is just another sign that
God is behind my little fundraiser. Women are now
buying me drinks right and left, touching my fingers
with their eyes, my crotch with their hands. My luck
is infallible and it's amazing. When suddenly I hear
this voice whispering in my head. "Roger," the voice
says, (At first I think it's Wayne Newton) Roger,
(That's my name)... "Go to the bathroom and do my
will." "—But I just went," I replied, "I don't need to
go." "—Don't argue!" the Voice repeats. "You know
who I am? This is God talking, just GO!" "—But I'm
winning a shitload here, God, and all in your name
too." "—Let it ride, he says, you just find your way
to the bathroom and sit in a stall till you can leave me
a real gift."
  So what can I do? I've been sitting here for two hours
now trying to do God's will and push this turtle out
while all my chips are out there riding the roulette
table. (grunts fiercely) Oh my god. I swear this is killing
me. Killing me! (Sighs.) Although I must say it's nice

to have someone to talk to at a time like this. Stranded on the toilet with nothing to show for it and not one fuckin sheet of toilet paper left on the roll.

DOCTOR PAYNE: Here.

(DOCTOR PAYNE *throws* ROGER *a fresh roll from a nearby stall.*)

ROGER: Thanks. I won't forget that. Not every day someone'll go out of their way to help you out like this. *(He wipes, flushes, then extends his hand.)* Name's Roger.

DOCTOR PAYNE: Might want to wash it first.

ROGER: Sorry.

DOCTOR PAYNE: *(Putting on a new latex glove, shakes hand.)* I'm Doctor Payne. William Payne. *(Hands him test tube with urine.)* Here. Hold this.

(ROGER *takes it.* DOCTOR PAYNE *lights a flame underneath it.)*

ROGER: *(Awestruck)* Cool.

DOCTOR PAYNE: Don't shake it! This urine seems to have an unusually high concentration of glycine.

ROGER: Sorry. *(Beat)* You know something, I think God wanted us to meet. Me and you. No accident you were here when I needed to wipe. And here I am helping you.

DOCTOR PAYNE: What are you talking about?

ROGER: I heard the Voice. Before. When I was out there gambling. First I thought it was Wayne Newton. But it was God. And he said: "Let the money ride. Go to the bathroom now. And let the money ride!" So I did. And I met you.

DOCTOR PAYNE: Don't you think you're reading too much into this?

ROGER: Oh no. There is always a reason if you're with God. Key is to keep all your options open. Receive all His divine messages in Hi-Def. And turn your heart into a beeper for His commands.

DOCTOR PAYNE: *(Sniffing test tube)* This is incredible! The inhibitory zone of this urine is more similar to ampicillin than anything else.

ROGER: Today I might wear a turban like Osama Bin Laden, tomorrow I might put on a yarmulka like the Pope. All depends on the work. And what God needs.

DOCTOR PAYNE: What about your three hundred thousand dollars? Wasn't that part of God's work too?

ROGER: Fuck the money. I told you. Important thing is I met you, Doc. Because you and me, we're a team now.

DOCTOR PAYNE: No. The important thing is the novel proteins I just discovered here. Isolated in the open air of these urinals, the antibacterial activity of these bioactive peptides has increased tenfold. Tenfold! Eureka! I think I may have just stumbled upon my ninth and final neo-plastin. Do you know what this means?! Do you know the implications?!

ROGER: Your fly is unzipped.

THE CONGRUENT SCIENCE OF COLLECTING MODERN ART

Scene 8

(DOCTOR PAYNE's *office.* RUTH *at her desk in the waiting room.* DOCTOR PAYNE *enters and hands her the thermos full of urine.)*

DOCTOR PAYNE: Please put this in the freezer, Ruth. And be careful not to spill a drop. *Not a drop!*

(RUTH *urgently whispers something to* DOCTOR PAYNE. *He can't make it out.)*

DOCTOR PAYNE: What...?

(RUTH *quickly writes something on scrap of paper, hands it to* DOCTOR PAYNE.

He reads her handwriting with difficulty.)

DOCTOR PAYNE: Who?

(RUTH *whispers in* DOCTOR PAYNE's *ear.)*

DOCTOR PAYNE: Where?

RUTH: Inside. From the F D A.

DOCTOR PAYNE: Your boyfirend...?

RUTH: Mister Freyberg. He's waiting in your office.

DOCTOR PAYNE: My—

RUTH: He had a warrant.

DOCTOR PAYNE: Fuck!

(Just then inner door to DOCTOR PAYNE's *office opens. And* DON *emerges. He's the one* DOCTOR PAYNE *has been actively trying to avoid.)*

DON: Doctor. I was wondering if you had a minute?

DOCTOR PAYNE: My five o'clock, right?

DON: Not exactly.

DOCTOR PAYNE: *(Glib)* No matter. What's time but a circular prison marked with numerals for bars?

(DOCTOR PAYNE ushers DON back into the medical room.)

DOCTOR PAYNE: Please sit and remove your shirt.

DON: Actually I'm with the Food and Drug Administration.

DOCTOR PAYNE: That doesn't make you immune. When was the last time you had a check up?

DON: That's not what I'm here for.

DOCTOR PAYNE: *(Sobering, dropping pretense)* I know why you came.

DON: So you remember me. Good. That should make things easier for us.

DOCTOR PAYNE: You have preconceptions. All of you. You come here with prejudice and envy in your heart.

DON: That's not—

DOCTOR PAYNE: *(Overlapping)* And the interest of those big pharmaceutical companies deep in your pockets.

DON: I work for the people.

DOCTOR PAYNE: Uh-huh.

DON: We are a government agency.

DOCTOR PAYNE: Oh I know who you are... what you are. The question is do you know who I am...? What I do. The world-shaking discovery I'm about to make. And the new cancer-free epoch I'm about to usher in.

DON: No, but that must explain why you've been so hard to pin down...

DOCTOR PAYNE: Don't get facetious with me, son. I'm not here to make you feel better about yourself. Look. Look around you. Do I look like some glorified mechanic who performs wholesale amputations? Some third world doctor who harvests organs from the city morgue? Am I chewing gum...? *(Sweeping gesture to his art)* Do these look like a bunch of screen savers to you?! No. These here are genuine Motherwells...Reinhardts, probably worth more than you'll make in a lifetime— and that includes winning the lottery. *(Beat)* You realize the vast history and tradition that had to be discarded before these paintings could ever be conceived or imagined. You think it's easy to be so random and carefree. I mean how do you compose randomness like this? Let alone *paint* it. These painted gestures are the broad strokes of life, my friend. No one cares about the crepuscular Flemish light pouring from some medieval window. Or the reclined nude bored shitless on her couch. Only the deeper more ineffable essence of life is recorded here. Which needless to say gives me a fuckin hardon just looking at it. *(Beat)* Now what do you think this one's called?

DON: Don't know.

DOCTOR PAYNE: Come on. Be bold. Take a risk.

DON: I'm not an art person.

DOCTOR PAYNE: Okay. I'll help you out. This is *Abstract Painting, Red.* And this?

DON: *Abstract Painting, Blue...?*

DOCTOR PAYNE: Very good. See, no tricks here.

DON: Look, I came to...

DOCTOR PAYNE: Last one. Come on. One more. *(Points)* My favorite. What's this one called?

DON: *(More confident)* Abstract Painting, White.

DOCTOR PAYNE: Bzzzz! WRONG! Gotcha! This one's called. *Untitled # 6*. Hahaha! Fuck if I know why, could've just as easily called it—*Christmas Memory #12* or *11*. But it's not. This is *Untitled #6*—and the name I'll have you know is an integral part of the abstraction. *(Beat)* But you know what I like most about Modern Art. I like that it's all about *showing* the mistakes. The mistakes become a vital part of the work. The process... Just like in research.

DON: Speaking of which...

DOCTOR PAYNE: *(Overriding)* So tell me. You think a man who appreciates all this, so *deeply*, would exploit his fellow man for something low and base as money...? That a doctor with such cultivated and refined tastes, would take advantage of the poor vulnerable state of his patients...?

DON: You don't seem to understand—

DOCTOR PAYNE: Oh but I think I do.

DON: No one is accusing you of anything.

DOCTOR PAYNE: Then why are you here? With a warrant. WHY?! Not for the art, I'm sure.

DON: When a doctor deviates from standard procedure, it is our job to...well, to perform a preliminary investigation.

DOCTOR PAYNE: *Preliminary* investigation...preliminary means the first step before those that are to follow. There are already fourteen counts issued against me. Seems to me like you are well on the way to a full-fledged inquisition here.

DON: I'm sorry, doctor, but having patients drink urine is not a viable cure in our book.

DOCTOR PAYNE: I'm thinking of going intravenous, if that helps assuage your complaint.

DON: That's not what I mean. You still have to run tests like everyone else.

DOCTOR PAYNE: But I am.

DON: With carefully kept records.

DOCTOR PAYNE: Call my patients any time you want. They'll be more than happy to testify on my behalf.

DON: I'm sure they will. Those that are alive. But I'm afraid personal anecdote is no substitute for hard data. The least you could do is agree to our clinical trials.

DOCTOR PAYNE: What?! And open myself up to your flawed interpretations... Never! I don't see Mother Theresa doing clinical trials? I should be feted and celebrated, but instead what do I get...I get mindless queries. Doubts. Detailed investigations. Prohibitive interdictions...? Accusations, aspersions, traducements... indictments. Have I missed anything here?

DON: You're doing it to yourself, doctor.

DOCTOR PAYNE: Why. Because I forgo publishing in your journals...? Refuse to submit to your trials?

DON: But a cure for cancer surely merits some attention. That's big news. *(Mocking, doubtful)* If you have indeed slain the dragon, doctor, it's your *obligation* to share it with the world. What's there to be so modest about?

DOCTOR PAYNE: Modest? *(Laughs)* I'm not modest, take my word for it. Hey Ruth!

RUTH: *(Entering)* Yes, doctor.

DOCTOR PAYNE: Am I modest.

RUTH: *(Chuckles)* No doctor. You're a genius. You've often told me so yourself.

DOCTOR PAYNE: Thank you Ruth.

*(*RUTH *exits.)*

DOCTOR PAYNE: One must trespass to transcend. *(He peers into his pants, reading)* "What doesn't kill me only makes me stronger." Einstein...Pasteur... those are the men we must first emulate. Then surpass. I'm just not ready yet. Not yet.

DON: And when will you be ready?

DOCTOR PAYNE: That's for me to decide.

DON: Don't you want to help others?

DOCTOR PAYNE: Yes. And you can help them too.

DON: Me...?

DOCTOR PAYNE: Let me do my work. Uninterrupted.

DON: I only want...

DOCTOR PAYNE: Unimpeded.

DON: ...to make sure—

DOCTOR PAYNE: Oh I know. Debunk me. Sweep me under the rug. Trust me I will prevail. The truth is on my side. But if

I publish before my time I will perish. There's a whole army out there of zealous detractors. A whole legion of "I told you so's..." eager to point their accusing fingers. No. I must be patient. Unyielding. And when I'm ready, only when I'm ready, can I go out. Not before. *(Beat)* Now let me listen to your chest.

DON: No. And far as you are concerned, you should consider lowering your public profile.

DOCTOR PAYNE: My public profile...

DON: T V appearances. Radio broadcasts. I don't think publicity is what you really want right now.

DOCTOR PAYNE: Is that so.

DON: I'd also refrain from seeing any new patients. Especially the more notable ones...

DOCTOR PAYNE: I'll try and keep that in mind as well.

DON: *(Overlapping)* Like Senator Cates.

DOCTOR PAYNE: How do you know about— Who told you about him?

DON: *(Overlapping)* I wouldn't rely on him too much, if I were you.

DOCTOR PAYNE: My patients are my own fuckin business!

DON: Just trying to give you a word of advice.

DOCTOR PAYNE: Get out.

DON: You're only making more trouble for yourself.

DOCTOR PAYNE: Get the fuck out!!

DON: I'll need validation.

DOCTOR PAYNE: What?

DON: *(Holds out parking ticket)* You do validate?

DOCTOR PAYNE: Do it yourself on the way out.

(Lights fade.)

DOCTOR PAYNE FORGOES THE LESSONS OF SCIENCE FOR THE ALECHEMY OF DESIRE IN A SCENE OF PERFECT LEVITATION

Scene 9

(DOCTOR PAYNE's bedroom. Late night. He watches T V, surfing channels—alternating between a porn station and an educational one. Absently masturbating without any goal or climax in sight.)

T V: *(Learning Channel)* The sperm swims up the fallopian tubes to encounter the egg...

(DOCTOR PAYNE switches back to porn flick.)

T V: *(Porn flick)* Oh fuck me...fuck me...shove your hard cock into my wet pussy...

(DOCTOR PAYNE switches again.)

T V: *(Learning Channel)* When the egg drops... it encounters the errant sperm that by some miracle, collides with it...

(Phone rings. DOCTOR PAYNE answers it, mutes T V.)

DOCTOR PAYNE: Hello? Who is it?

(Lights up on Ms Yankovich, the MOTHER, on phone. She is bathed in the light of her own T V.)

MOTHER: It's me, Ms Yankovich.

DOCTOR PAYNE: How did you get my home phone?

MOTHER: I need to see you.

DOCTOR PAYNE: You know what time it is?

MOTHER: My son is worse. Not better. Worse.

DOCTOR PAYNE: Relax. Dosage probably wasn't high enough. Just need to double the dosage.

MOTHER: I need to come in first thing in the morning.

DOCTOR PAYNE: I've got therapy in the morning.
Can't make it till noon.

MOTHER: What should I do till then? *(She coughs.)*
You have to see me.

DOCTOR PAYNE: Maybe you should have that cough
looked at.

MOTHER: It's nothing. Just from crying.

DOCTOR PAYNE: *(Slightly aroused)* Maybe another X-ray.
Free of charge.

MOTHER: Tell me what to do. I need to do something.
Anything.

DOCTOR PAYNE: What channel are you watching?

MOTHER: Excuse me?

DOCTOR PAYNE: In the background. I can hear your T V.
What channel?

MOTHER: I'm on 36—the Christian station—but it might
be different in your neighborhood. *(Beat)* Help my son.
Please.

DOCTOR PAYNE: Just make sure he's well hydrated and
comfortable.

MOTHER: Wait. Don't hang up. *(Beat)* Have you ever
watched a child in pain, Doctor? If you've ever watched
your own child suffering, like I am doing now, then
you'd know how I feel. The way they come to you for
help and comfort that you can't give them. No matter
how hard you try. So instead you keep promising to
ease their pain—*Shhh...it'll get better, shhh, soon it'll be
all gone*—your empty promise like a present you can't
afford to buy. It's unimaginable. This torture. And the
agony of those who must witness this pain. There's no

need for children to suffer in this world. Tell me,
what have they ever done? What?!

DOCTOR PAYNE: And the sins of the parents shall
be visited on the children...

MOTHER: But I haven't done anything. Not to deserve
something like this. Not even in my past lives.

DOCTOR PAYNE: Of course not, but you should have
come to me first. I get much better results before they
get contaminated with chemo and radiation.

MOTHER: I didn't know, I...

DOCTOR PAYNE: Can he sit? Can you get him to sit?

MOTHER: He can barely lie down.

DOCTOR PAYNE: See if you can get him to sit.

(MOTHER *tries,* YURI *collapses. Tries again)*

MOTHER: Should I pray?

DOCTOR PAYNE: Might as well, what harm can it do.
Now goodnight.

(DOCTOR PAYNE *hangs up. Picks up remote and changes
channel—from porn fucking: "Look how big and hard you
got" —to religious channel—where an evangelist preaches.)*

T V: *(Religious station)* The Lord shall heal and preserve
you. With righteous rectitude you shall follow his
ways and He, in turn, will inhabit you with his love.
Hallelujah!!

(On other side of stage, MOTHER *and* YURI *watch this as
well. Praying with Jesus)*

MOTHER: God, if you can help them, you can help me.
Help my son sit.

(DOCTOR PAYNE *stands and drops his pants. Stares at T V.
At his own prick.)*

DOCTOR PAYNE: *(Shouting at his penis)* Up you lazy sonofabitch. Up! You're getting no helping hand from me tonight. Up!

T V: *(Religious station)* This is the power of God. He will heal and protect you. hallelujah! He will lift your sorrows and levitate your soul.

DOCTOR PAYNE: Up!! You miserable cunt of a cock. Up! You pussy. UP!

(DOCTOR PAYNE raises his arms high above his head, as if in some prayer....an epiphanic gesture of total surrender. Tries to levitate his penis without hands as he stares hard between his own legs.)

DOCTOR PAYNE: Get up you sonofabitch. Up!

MOTHER: Dear God please help him sit up. I beg you please.

DOCTOR PAYNE: UP!!! UP!! UP!!! *(He begins laughing to himself. Or is it crying.)*

(On T V the preacher has also raised his arms. Congregation sways in unison.)

(MOTHER raises her arms too.)

(Each enraptured in their own way.)

DOCTOR PAYNE	MOTHER:
Hallelujah!	Hallelujah!

(Lights fade)

THE INTERPRETATION OF UNDREAMT DREAMS

Scene 10

(Psychiatrist's office. DOCTOR PAYNE *sits silently, staring intently ahead.* THERAPIST *waits expectantly.*

THERAPIST: Everything okay?

DOCTOR PAYNE: Sure. Why not.

THERAPIST: You know, they say pain is not just a physical experience, but also an emotional one.

*(*DOCTOR PAYNE *grunts.)*

THERAPIST: You're very quiet today. Haven't said a word.

DOCTOR PAYNE: I'm looking at your couch.

THERAPIST: You can lie down if you want.

DOCTOR PAYNE: The pillows are all ruffled.

THERAPIST: Yes...

DOCTOR PAYNE: Did the patient before me lie down?

THERAPIST: *(Coyly deflecting)* Maybe.

DOCTOR PAYNE: You like them more than me... or am I your favorite?

THERAPIST: You know I can't answer that.

DOCTOR PAYNE: Okay then am I your most *interesting* patient...?

THERAPIST: Certainly my most...challenging.

DOCTOR PAYNE: Is that why you like me less than everyone else?

THERAPIST: I never said that.

DOCTOR PAYNE: *(Overlapping)* Would you like me *more* if I lay down?

THERAPIST: Please. This isn't—

DOCTOR PAYNE: Why can't I be your favorite?

THERAPIST: You know I can't answer that.

DOCTOR PAYNE: Relax. I was just kidding anyway. I don't care if you like me or not. What I care about is why in the world would anyone ever want to lie down in the first place?

THERAPIST: It has its advantages.

DOCTOR PAYNE: Convince me.

THERAPIST: When you lie down you avoid eye contact... this allows you to focus more on your inner thoughts. Supposed to be a lot more *associative* in its evocations.

DOCTOR PAYNE: But I like eye contact. See what I'm up against.

THERAPIST: You sure you don't want to give it a try?

DOCTOR PAYNE: Fuck no. Day I lie down is day I'm dead.

THERAPIST: Okay. But in my professional opinion, your harsh protest and denial only betrays a real interest in doing so.

DOCTOR PAYNE: And in my professional opinion, your professional opinion is shit. Tell me, was the patient before me male or female?

THERAPIST: I'm sorry, but I can't divulge that.

DOCTOR PAYNE: No, of course not. You know, I don't think I could ever be a therapist. Get a female patient lying on that couch and—WHAM!—it would be all over in a matter of seconds. How do you do it, doctor?

THERAPIST: I don't consider my patients in that way.

DOCTOR PAYNE: Really? Why not?

THERAPIST: When I come here it's work.

DOCTOR PAYNE: Is that all I am to you...? Work?

THERAPIST: Has something changed in your life since the last time we met?

DOCTOR PAYNE: Changed?

THERAPIST: You seem overall more needy today?

DOCTOR PAYNE: Me?

THERAPIST: More...*vulnerable.*

DOCTOR PAYNE: I'm not vulnerable. What makes you think I'm vulnerable. Just because I refuse to lie down. Fuck vulnerable!

THERAPIST: That wasn't meant pejoratively.

DOCTOR PAYNE: *Never be vulnerable!* You must at all times make yourself impervious to sickness and infirmity. NEVER BE VULNERABLE!

THERAPIST: *(Beat)* Yes, well... What about your dreams?

DOCTOR PAYNE: What?

THERAPIST: Any new dreams? Blood...?

DOCTOR PAYNE: Nothing worth repeating really.

THERAPIST: Sometimes those are the most important ones.

DOCTOR PAYNE: I doubt it.

THERAPIST: They say you dream for your therapist.

DOCTOR PAYNE: Oh yeah?

THERAPIST: You know you'll be coming here to see me, so in light of that knowledge, knowing I'll be a receptive audience to your needs, you have a certain

kind of dream you might not otherwise have had.
Something the two of us can then share and discuss.

DOCTOR PAYNE: Are you saying my dream is a kind
of *present* to you?

THERAPIST: In a manner of speaking...yes.

DOCTOR PAYNE: A *gift*...?

THERAPIST: And my interpretation is my reciprocal gift
back to you.

DOCTOR PAYNE: Okay. Fine. Then why do you hate me
so much?

THERAPIST: I don't hate you.

DOCTOR PAYNE: All my life people have been repulsed
by me. I can tell. No one says it to my face, but deep
down I know. Even you...

THERAPIST: I never said—

DOCTOR PAYNE: *(Overlapping)* Or the F D A for
example. What do they want with me? They're all
out to get me. The whole world. And despite that—
no, because of that—I will succeed. I refuse to show
weakness. And people hate that. They really do.

THERAPIST: I'm not saying you're paranoid, but have
you ever considered the possibility that you actually
create these enemies in order to feed your fear of
success?

DOCTOR PAYNE: That's ridiculous. People don't like
me because I am a fuckwad. Plain and simple. Truth
is I don't even like myself much.

THERAPIST: O K. Back to your dream...

DOCTOR PAYNE: My...?

THERAPIST: Go on. Tell me whatever you remember.
(She sits poised with pen over a notebook.)

(DOCTOR PAYNE *stands, paces. Says nothing. Then stops at couch. Lies down*)

DOCTOR PAYNE: You mind...?

THERAPIST: Please.

(DOCTOR PAYNE *gets comfortable on couch. Adjusting pillows.*)

DOCTOR PAYNE: Do I take my shoes off?

THERAPIST: Up to you.

DOCTOR PAYNE: Make sure to wake me if I fall asleep. Don't want to be paying for overtime at these rates. (*Awkward laugh*) Hahaha...

THERAPIST: (*Sobering*) I'll let you know.

DOCTOR PAYNE: You ever wonder what doctors did before anesthesia was discovered...? How they performed their professional butchery with all that kicking and screaming? Later, with the advent of anesthesia, cutting up a patient was like buying your meat at the supermarket. The carnage was now disguised and sanitized, all wrapped and palatable as the screaming was put on mute and a certain passivity crept into the operation... Now the trust of sleep was deposited entirely in the hands of the good doctor... But *not* the dreams. No. The dreams had to wait for psychoanalysts. Like you. That was their meat and *blood*. Am I right?

THERAPIST: I'm still waiting for yours doctor.

DOCTOR PAYNE: Okay. Okay. But don't' blame me if you're bored. My dreams all seem so tame in daylight. So mundane and pedestrian.

THERAPIST: Like I said, those can be the most meaningful sometimes.

(DOCTOR PAYNE *adjusts himself on the couch.*)

DOCTOR PAYNE: Not bad. This lying down business... not bad at all.

THERAPIST: See, you never can tell till you try something.

DOCTOR PAYNE: Oh I can tell. *(Kicks off shoes, adjusts pillow)* I can tell that from this angle, on the couch, I have a clean unobstructed view right between your legs doctor. And who in the world would've guessed that you'd be wearing a thong during that time of the month. Really very risky of you. With that heavy blood flow. But then again, blood is nothing once it leaves the body. Is it?

*(*THERAPIST *angrily gets up to go.)*

DOCTOR PAYNE: Hey, don't you want to hear my dream?

*(*THERAPIST *stares at* DOCTOR PAYNE.)*

DOCTOR PAYNE: My gift...?

THERAPIST: You are truly a repulsive man.

(Lights fade.)

THE MOMENTARY TRANSFIGURATION OF DOCTOR PAYNE BY A DESPERATE WOMAN WHO WILL DO ANYTHING...AND DOES

Scene 11

*(*DOCTOR PAYNE's *office. He enters in a good mood, cradling a wrapped package—painting—under his arm, unaware that something is going on.)*

DOCTOR PAYNE: Good morning, Ruth. Gooooood Morning. Wait till you see what I got. Ta Da!

RUTH: Looks like another X-ray, Doctor.

DOCTOR PAYNE: Come on, Ruthie. You know better than that. *This* is ART. Any asshole can *buy* art; I *acquire* it.

(A GOVERNMENT MAN *walks past* DOCTOR PAYNE *carrying several cardboard boxes.)*

GOVERNMENT MAN: Excuse me.

DOCTOR PAYNE: Hey, where are you going with that? *(To* RUTH*)* What's going on here, Ruth? Who is that?

GOVERNMENT MAN: Sorry that's government property now.

RUTH: I tried to stop them doctor.

DOCTOR PAYNE: What the hell's going on in here!?

RUTH: I tried to call you, Doctor. But your batteries must be dead again.

DOCTOR PAYNE: They can't do this. Hey you! Stop that!

*(*DOCTOR PAYNE *tries to enter the inner office but is intercepted by* GOVERNMENT MAN.*)*

GOVERNMENT MAN: I'm sorry, you can't go in there.

DOCTOR PAYNE: What the fuck is going on here? This is *my* office.

*(*DON, *the F D A man, now appears in the door with a checklist.)*

DON: *(Matter of fact, but cruel)* We're confiscating all your papers, Doc.

DOCTOR PAYNE: Like fuck you are. You can't to that. *(To* RUTH*)* They can't do that.

DON: If you wouldn't mind waiting outside we should be done in a few minutes, Doctor Payne.

DOCTOR PAYNE: I need those charts. My patient's histories. I need—

DON: So do we.

DOCTOR PAYNE: I can't treat my patients without those papers. My patients will die if I can't treat them.

*(Just then—*MOTHER *comes in. Tries to get* DOCTOR PAYNE'*s attention to no avail.)*

DON: I'm sorry. But I urged you to apply for clinical trials.

DOCTOR PAYNE: *(Through his teeth)* Oh yeah, you little bureaucratic suckbutt. We'll see who's got the last word here. Ruth! Get me Senator Cates on the line.

(RUTH *dials.)*

DOCTOR PAYNE: *(To* DON*)* I hope you like the mailroom, because by the time I'm through with you, licking envelopes will be the closest you'll ever get to kissing ass.

(Finding a brief moment, MOTHER *finally grabs* DOCTOR PAYNE'*s arm.)*

MOTHER: Doctor. Thank god you are here, Doctor. I've been calling and calling...

DOCTOR PAYNE: Not now. Not Now! Ruth take care of her. I'm performing triage here.

MOTHER: *(To* RUTH*)* But the doctor told me to come by this afternoon.

RUTH: Just a minute dear.

MOTHER: It's an emergency. He told me— Last night—

RUTH: So's this.

MOTHER: But I must—

RUTH: He'll take care of you soon as he can.

(GOVERNMENT MAN *crosses with another box.)*

GOVERNMENT MAN: Don, you want the box of X-rays as well.

DON: Everything. I want everything.

DOCTOR PAYNE: Jesus!! Not my X-rays. You don't need the X-rays. Please!!

DON: *(With relish)* Everything goes.

GOVERNMENT MAN: *(Disgusted, suspicious)* Some of 'em are stuck together.

DON: *(Vindictive)* Everything except the art work. Artwork can stay. I don't give a fuck about that priceless degenerate shit. You can leave all that for the good doctor to enjoy.

DOCTOR PAYNE: What's taking so long, Ruth? Is the Senator there?

RUTH: No one's answering.

MOTHER: *(Urgently)* Doctor.

DOCTOR PAYNE: *(Tearing free)* Hold on!!

DOCTOR PAYNE: Try his cell phone. Now!

DON: I'm afraid the Senator can't be disturbed, Doc.

DOCTOR PAYNE: Fuck you, Dan!

DON: Don. Don Freydburg. *(Beat)* And for your information, the Senator is in the middle of delivering a very important filibuster...on your behalf apparently. Something about re-vamping alternative medicine. Isn't that supreme irony...? While he's there trying to make changes on your behalf, we took the opportunity to help you tidy your office. That's why we came here. At this auspicious moment. To visit with you now. This very hour.

DOCTOR PAYNE: You fuck! I hope you get inoperable gliobastoma...and I'm the only one with the antidote.

DON: If you need access to papers you can always come xerox them at our office any time between nine and twelve...at your own cost of course. So bring lots of quarters.

DOCTOR PAYNE: This is bullshit. BULLSHIT!

MOTHER: Doctor Payne...my son...you told me...

DOCTOR PAYNE: *(Exploding)* What the fuck is it?!

MOTHER: You told me to come see you this afternoon.

DOCTOR PAYNE: Can't you see I'm in a crisis?!

MOTHER: But my son.

DOCTOR PAYNE: This isn't a good time.

RUTH: I tried to tell her.

MOTHER: I need to talk to you.

DOCTOR PAYNE: Later!

MOTHER: He's getting worse.

DOCTOR PAYNE: Take him to Disneyland. What the fuck do I care?! Better yet, Michael Jackson is always looking for new guests at his *Neverland* ranch.

MOTHER: Please. I think he's dying. Last night. You told me to come here today...last night.

DOCTOR PAYNE: You see that man by the door.

(DOCTOR PAYNE *points to* DON, *who's getting ready to exit.*)

DOCTOR PAYNE: He's the one killing your son. Not me. You want to save your son... go talk to him.

(As MOTHER *crosses to* DON—DOCTOR PAYNE *storms into his inner office, slams door.*)

DOCTOR PAYNE: Fuck fuck fuck!

MOTHER: *(To* DON*)* Excuse me, sir. Sir...?

DON: *(Dismissive)* Not now, ma'am. Not now. *(He exits.)*

*(*MOTHER *cries.* RUTH *goes to comfort her.)*

(Inside the inner office, on other side of door, DOCTOR PAYNE *is busy cursing.)*

DOCTOR PAYNE: My beloved X-rays.... What the fuck right have they to take my fuckin beloved X-rays?! Fuck you fuck you fuck you.

(Timid knock on door)

DOCTOR PAYNE: Who the fuck is it?

MOTHER: You told me to come in the afternoon.

DOCTOR PAYNE: That was last night. Before this— Get out! I'm busy—

MOTHER: My son.

DOCTOR PAYNE: Nothing personal. But fuck your son. I'm having a really shitty day here. And I don't feel like being nice to anyone.

MOTHER: You promised to help me.

DOCTOR PAYNE: Look at this place. You still think I'm the one to help your son? Place is a shambles.

MOTHER: Where else can I go?

DOCTOR PAYNE: Great! Faith by default. How inspiring.

MOTHER: My son is worse since we came here.

DOCTOR PAYNE: That's life.

MOTHER: You promised you could help me.

DOCTOR PAYNE: I said I'd try. Now go. Poof!

*(*MOTHER *doesn't budge. So* DOCTOR PAYNE *hastily scribbles something down and hands it to her.)*

DOCTOR PAYNE: Okay, here's a new prescription. Good bye.

(MOTHER *still doesn't leave.* DOCTOR PAYNE *turns on her.*)

DOCTOR PAYNE: What?! I don't perform miracles. I just
try my best. I told you that on the first day.

MOTHER: *(Holds out prescription)* I don't have money for
this.

DOCTOR PAYNE: No money.

MOTHER: I used it all on the first round of medicine and
that didn't help.

DOCTOR PAYNE: What about insurance? Surely you
must have—

MOTHER: Expired.

DOCTOR PAYNE: *(Overlapping)* That's not good. You
don't have money, I can't very well help you. Research
costs money. I need payment up front. You see the kind
of obstacles I must face. The lawsuits I'm forced to
litigate.

MOTHER: Please.

DOCTOR PAYNE: Casinos may feed you for free, but
that's only so you'd gamble more efficiently. There's
a responsibility involved here that you seem quite eager
to overlook.

MOTHER: I'll find the money. I promise. It's just that—

DOCTOR PAYNE: Hey, I don't mind, I'm as generous
and munificent as the next fuck but it's all my other
patients I'm thinking about. If I were to help you, *gratis*,
how would that help them? In not paying me you're
essentially depriving all my other patients as well.
And that's just not fair.

MOTHER: You think I'm holding back from you?!
My son's life is at stake. And you think I'm trying
to hold back.

DOCTOR PAYNE: You'd be surprised what some people would do.

MOTHER: Believe me, doctor, if I could make his sickness mine, I'd happily do it. I'd do anything to save my child. Anything.

DOCTOR PAYNE: But you still look healthy enough.

MOTHER: I do not understand—

DOCTOR PAYNE: You say you'd help your son if you could...dress yourself with his pain if it fit you. And yet there are a lot of people less healthy than you... whom you could still help.

MOTHER: I...

DOCTOR PAYNE: *(Overlapping)* Certain sacrifices you could still make.

MOTHER: But I have—

DOCTOR PAYNE: *(Overriding)* God provided us with two hands so we could offer one to a friend in need.

MOTHER: I don't see—

DOCTOR PAYNE: *(Overlapping)* Two *lungs*, two *kidneys*...there are things you can do...give... to help your son by helping others.

MOTHER: Are you suggesting I sell one of my organs, Doctor...? Is that what you're saying?

DOCTOR PAYNE: Do you believe in sacrifice, Ms Yankovich? *(Pause)* Money after all is just another a form of sacrifice...something we substitute for something else... for something we need. If you were so inclined I could give you a few numbers to call. Help you sacrifice what is not needed. People in Istanbul do it all the time. It would help settle some debt. Without really compromising your own health of course.

MOTHER: You think I haven't thought of all that?

DOCTOR PAYNE: I don't know...how desperate are you?

(MOTHER *lifts her shirt to show* DOCTOR PAYNE *a scar. He runs his hand along it, lovingly, lingering, aroused.*)

DOCTOR PAYNE: Mmm...well...maybe there's other ways, Mrs Yankovich. Yes, maybe there are other ways to continue with your son's treatment. *(Tracing the scar)* Did you know that skin is the largest organ in the human body? Right now. Touching you here, like this, I'm touching you everywhere.

MOTHER: Oh Lord please help me do the right thing.

DOCTOR PAYNE: Now obviously I know I'm *not* God, not really, not in the strict definition of the word. He makes people, I just fix them. But even so...let me ask you a simple question.

MOTHER: Please help my son!!

DOCTOR PAYNE: Would you suck my dick?

MOTHER: I...

DOCTOR PAYNE: You don't have to swallow. Just suck.

MOTHER: I...

DOCTOR PAYNE: Although it can't hurt to swallow.

MOTHER: If it could help him. If you thought it might help.

(DOCTOR PAYNE *hands* MOTHER *the wig that* RUTH *wore earlier.*)

DOCTOR PAYNE: Here. Try this on. *(Beat)* You are not the only one to have suffered loss. Have I already told you that you resemble my dead wife?

(*As* MOTHER *dons the wig,* DOCTOR PAYNE *hangs his new Motherwell on the wall. Again steps back to appraise painting. She adjusts wig.*)

DOCTOR PAYNE: *(Re painting)* What do you think...?
Helps calm the spirit, doesn't it? The balance of black
and white in a world of meaningless color.

*(MOTHER shrugs approvingly. DOCTOR PAYNE adjusts the
painting once more, then adjusts her newly donned wig.)*

DOCTOR PAYNE: Good. Now let's get to work.

(DOCTOR PAYNE unzips. MOTHER gets on her knees.)

MOTHER: Save my son. Please.

DOCTOR PAYNE: *(Lifts hands up aloft)* I'll do my best.

MOTHER: Thank you. Thank you god.

(Lights fade.)

THE ARCHEOLOGY OF GOD'S ACCIDENT JUST WAITING TO BE UNEARTHED

Scene 12

*(Casino. DOCTOR PAYNE is gambling intently, drinking
heavily, very heavily—when ROGER approaches.*

ROGER: Wow! Looks like someone's winning large here.
Know what they say don't you— "Lucky in cards,
unlucky in love." And judging from what I see, I'd
say your love life must be really fucked. Am I right?
Am I right?

(DOCTOR PAYNE is about to take another card from dealer.)

ROGER: I wouldn't do that. The Voice says you should
split those ladies and double down.

DOCTOR PAYNE: The Voice...?

ROGER: Mind if I keep you company?

DOCTOR PAYNE: Actually I feel like being alone right
now.

ROGER: That's when you need it most. *(He sits.)* Just so you know, I haven't left my room since the last time I saw you. Been waiting for God's sign the whole time. Ordering grilled cheese from room service and watching cable T V. I don't know who does their programming but I swear it's like one big Holocaust festival up there. *Sophie's Choice, The Pianist, Schindler's List*... I think they're trying to drive you *out* of the room and *into* the casino. But it backfired with me. I got addicted to the stuff. Watched *Boys From Brazil* four times. Someone should really do a study about luck and the Holocaust. Those that survived and those that didn't. Anyway, I think I might be one of those lost Boys I really do... My father died when he was sixty-five, you know, just like Hitler. Then today, as I'm practicing my salute in the mirror, the Voice suddenly returns. I looked out my window and there's this electronic billboard with the Blue Men talking on it. Who needs a burning bush when you've got the Blue Man whispering right outside your window. So I leave my room for the first time in Godknowshowlong and *guess* who I run into but you. *Boy, I'm glad to see you again!* How have you been?

DOCTOR PAYNE: Do I know you?

ROGER: I'm Roger. Remember me? You gave me that roll of toilet paper. In the bathroom. Had this nice thermos with you. With Mickey on the side.

DOCTOR PAYNE: You know how cancer works...?

ROGER: It kills you. *(More laughter)*

DOCTOR PAYNE: Only towards the end. Before that. At the very beginning, everyone's getting along great and the body welcomes this new guest like some long lost friend, feeding it, providing cheap lodging, even deploying a fresh network of capillaries to allow for its guest's rapid growth. See...the body is eager to be liked and so it ingratiates itself to this new guest. Introducing this cancer to other nearby organs and then along the *circulatory autobahn*— Hi everybody, this is mutant cell X—Please say hello and be nice.

ROGER: Are you trying to tell me something here?

DOCTOR PAYNE: *(To dealer)* I'll take two. *(To* ROGER*)* Yes. Goodbye.

ROGER: What's the matter, doc? Not good enough to patronize with the likes of me except in the men's toilet?

DOCTOR PAYNE: *(He folds)* Shit!

ROGER: You and I, we're a lot more alike than you'd think. Here. Check this out. But be careful cause the ink's still wet. *(He sidles close to* DOCTOR PAYNE*, and pulls out his pants waistline. Reads.)* GOD FORGIVES THE UNREPENTANT. Got the idea when I saw you shaking yours at the urinal. Except mine's in English.

DOCTOR PAYNE: *(Sarcastic)* I'm flattered.

ROGER: For a while I considered tattooing— "GOD EVEN LOVES THOSE WHO DON'T LOVE HIM." But I'm afraid I didn't have enough real estate to fit all the words in, if you know what I mean...

DOCTOR PAYNE: *(Histrionic)* Shhh! Do you hear it?

ROGER: What?

DOCTOR PAYNE: The Voice. I think it's talking again.

ROGER: You too?

DOCTOR PAYNE: *(Ghostly, histrionic)* It's saying: "Get lost, Roger. Go home and leave the fuckin Doctor alone!"

ROGER: Very funny. Hahhaha. Very funny. Do you believe in accidents...?

DOCTOR PAYNE: I believe that's my drink you're drinking.

ROGER: Fuck, I'm sorry. Let me buy you another. Waitress!

DOCTOR PAYNE: Forget it.

ROGER: *(Overlap)* Because I don't.

DOCTOR PAYNE: What?

ROGER: Believe in accidents. You winning like this. Me sitting here next to you. Talking the way we're talking.

DOCTOR PAYNE: *(Insert, accusatory)* I'm not talking.

ROGER: *Listening.* It's all the same for God. Nothing's an accident in his eyes. *(Beat)* Do you believe in God?

DOCTOR PAYNE: Not unless it's an accident.

ROGER: So what do you believe in?

DOCTOR PAYNE: Disease. Death. Spanish Influenza of 1918. And, right now, the Three of Clubs.

ROGER: That's very cynical, wouldn't you say?

DOCTOR PAYNE: I'm a doctor, what do you expect? *(He empties glass.)* Last week this six year old boy came to get an M R I. Ironically they made him remove the large metal cross from around his neck...but neglected to see that someone left an oxygen tank by *accident* in the corner of the room. *(He peeks at his cards.)* Well, soon as the enormous imaging magnet was flicked on, the powerful magnet sucked the heavy oxygen tank like a paper clip from across the room and SMASHED it against the poor boy's head, killing him instantly in what came to be known as...*a freak accident*. But in fact, the elements for this putative accident were there in the room all along, unrehearsed, just waiting to ambush the boy at the precise intersection of when he lay down and when the machine was switched on. You see, the

accident was not an accident at all, only a hidden
moment of history expressing itself unannounced.
(He trades some cards.)

ROGER: How do you know God wasn't working the
G P S on that one?

DOCTOR PAYNE: God or no God, doesn't matter what
you call it, these things are always there ready to
happen. Not just *the little six year-old boy with his
fractured skull*—but also the more veiled accidents
developing inside us. Like the p51 gene for example...
or that one cell that refuses to self-terminate... or the
other more ambitious ones that won't stop multiplying.
We are always so shocked to hear when cancer has been
found or detected. "Oh, I can't believe it. They're so
young. Or in such good health." But truth is, when
you consider the body is made up of thirty trillion cells,
thirty fuckin trillion cells, and each cell is occupied with
its very own cycle, well, that's a pretty overwhelming
deck to deal from—and in my humble opinion, it's a
fuckin wonder that cancer is not more prevalent than
it is. *That's* the real *accident* if you stop to think about it.
That there are not *more* accidents out there every
minute of the day. In fact, it's kind of a *miracle* when
you think about it. *(Folds cards)* Shit!

ROGER: Why did you become a doctor then?

DOCTOR PAYNE: Truth...? I liked being able to touch
other people without having to be touched back.

ROGER: What about helping them...you like helping
people?

DOCTOR PAYNE: Christ! I'm trying but they won't let
me! *They won't let me!*

ROGER: Who? Who won't let you.

DOCTOR PAYNE: Who do you think?

ROGER: The Zionists...?

DOCTOR PAYNE: No. The F DA. They're trying to shut me down.

ROGER: Now that's no accident! No accident at all. But you'd be surprised how easy it is to *fix* these so-called accidents when you have a mind to.

DOCTOR PAYNE: I've got to be at federal court early in the morning.

ROGER: *(Impressed)* No shit. You want me to come with you. I could be your bodyguard.

DOCTOR PAYNE: Thanks, but I'll manage just fine.

ROGER: You know, I was at the gun show last month. You're welcome to borrow anything in my arsenal if you want. A Ruger Mini-14, some semi-automatic rifles, a few Mossberg shotguns, Beretta 9MM pistols...got it all for under seven grand. That's a pretty amazing deal when you stop and think about it.

DOCTOR PAYNE: I'll be okay.

ROGER: I'm sure you will. But if you change your mind—

DOCTOR PAYNE: —I'll let you know. Now if you don't mind, I'd like to get back to my game.

ROGER: I hope you don't think you've been losing because of me.

DOCTOR PAYNE: What would ever make me think that?

ROGER: Because that would really hurt my feelings.

(Lights fade.)

LIKE NOAH AND JACOB BEFORE HIM, THE DOCTOR SHAMELESSLY PLEADS FOR A HATEFUL HUMANITY

Scene 13

*(Still in his lab coat, somewhat hung over—*DOCTOR PAYNE *is addressing an unseen jury. Part dream/part real.)*

DOCTOR PAYNE: LADIES AND GENTLEMEN OF THE JURY
Although I do not consider this a legitimate court,
I have nonetheless decided to represent myself here
before you—not for my sake—but for that of my
patients. By denying me free access to my work you
have in effect sentenced my patients to a double death:
first with cancer, and now with your interdiction
against their last hope for a cure. It is for them and
them alone that I stand here today. Certainly not
your judgment. Keep your stupid Nobel Prize and
Guggenheims if you must... just let me finish my work.
I beg you. Because I know I'm close. Oh so close. Closer
than ever before in my life.

(Singing starts offstage.)

DOCTOR PAYNE: In fact just the other night I had the
strangest dream, a dream where I was curing my
patients with the gift of song. That's right, overnight
I had become this incredible *chanteuse*.... My voice
suddenly finding perfect resonance with the cloying
disease of my patients, shattering their tumors like a
wine glass, and healing them with the tender touch of
my voice as I sung my fucking heart out. But now it's
daylight again, and I've forgotten the song let alone the
melody that gave it strength. *(He opens his mouth to sing.*

A long mournful note escapes, it lasts longer than humanly possible.)

(Lights fade.)

A CLEAR CASE OF MISDIAGNOSIS DEALT BY THE FICKLE HAND OF FATE

Scene 14

(DOCTOR PAYNE's office. Barren. White. No art. All the files have been removed. Cupboards emptied. He is consulting with the SENATOR CATES.)

SENATOR CATES: You redecorating, Doc?

DOCTOR PAYNE: *(Overlapping)* I need my files back.

SENATOR CATES: Court will deliver judgment in a week on the outside.

DOCTOR PAYNE: You have to help me. I can't work like this.

SENATOR CATES: I'll have everything back to normal and better. But first I want to see my latest X-ray.

(DOCTOR PAYNE produces an X-ray, shares it with SENATOR CATES.)

SENATOR CATES: So what exactly am I looking at here?

DOCTOR PAYNE: Good news. That's what. Very good news.

SENATOR CATES: And the diarrhea?

DOCTOR PAYNE: That's good news too. Means the tumor is dissolving. Like some practiced coin trick I've made it disappear.

SENATOR CATES: Now you see it, now you don't.

DOCTOR PAYNE: That's right. Your diarrhea is simply the waste product of your tumor.

SENATOR CATES: How do I know it's not just another side-effect of the medicine?

DOCTOR PAYNE: You don't. But if you look at the X-ray more carefully, you'll note a marked improvement.

SENATOR CATES: How marked?

DOCTOR PAYNE: You are very suspicious Senator. Would you rather receive a poor diagnosis? Would *that* make you feel better?

SENATOR CATES: No...but it's just that I've had a very strange morning so far. Dogs barking everywhere I go. Black birds circling the sky over my head. Something's not right today.

DOCTOR PAYNE: Maybe you should've gone to see a fortuneteller instead of coming here.

SENATOR CATES: Be careful, Doc. You're arrogance has won you a lot of enemies up on the hill.

DOCTOR PAYNE: What can I say, I'd rather jerk off than kiss ass.

SENATOR CATES: Let me see that X-ray again.

DOCTOR PAYNE: It's not a college diploma.

SENATOR CATES: You sure this is better?

DOCTOR PAYNE: A roadmap to health, Senator. Just look at those unobstructed capillaries—that there is a clear path to recovery.

SENATOR CATES: Excellent. *(Takes out a pack of cigarettes)* Does that mean I can smoke?

DOCTOR PAYNE: Smoking, you should know, leads to impotency.

SENATOR CATES: One thing at a time, doctor. One thing at a time. *(He lights up in* DOCTOR PAYNE's *office.)*

(The MOTHER, *Ms Yankovich, barges in.)*

DOCTOR PAYNE: Jesus! I'm in the middle of a meeting....

RUTH: I'm sorry, doctor. She wouldn't listen.

*(*DOCTOR PAYNE *motions* RUTH *to call security.)*

DOCTOR PAYNE: Look if it's about the bill, you should discuss it with Ruth out front.

MOTHER: My son...

DOCTOR PAYNE: Yes...I know.

MOTHER: He died.

DOCTOR PAYNE: I'm sorry. But these things are expected.

MOTHER: I swallowed and he died.

DOCTOR PAYNE: I really am sorry....

MOTHER: That wasn't supposed to happen. It wasn't—

DOCTOR PAYNE: I told you "No Guarantees". I'm not God.

MOTHER: You promised.

DOCTOR PAYNE: I promised I'd try. No one else was even willing to do that. Were they? WERE THEY?!

MOTHER: You took advantage of me.

DOCTOR PAYNE: Only with your consent.

MOTHER: When god wouldn't help me, I decided to see the devil...I should've stuck with god.

DOCTOR PAYNE: He'd still be dead.

MOTHER: You evil man!

DOCTOR PAYNE: I'm sorry, but I'm with a patient right now. If you want I'd be willing to negotiate a reduction in the bill. But that's as far as I'll go. I will not share in your pity. Not when I've done my best. Not when you've had the best.

MOTHER: I want my son back.

DOCTOR PAYNE: I'm afraid I have other patients here. Ruth, where's security?!

MOTHER: You make him come back. Bring him back!

DOCTOR PAYNE: If I hear anything I'll call. But you can always try cloning in the meantime.

(Guard comes in and escorts MOTHER *out.)*

DOCTOR PAYNE: Goodbye Mrs. Yankovich

SENATOR CATES: Not a happy customer.

DOCTOR PAYNE: Customers pay. This was charity. Besides, she came too late. Wouldn't follow orders.

SENATOR CATES: I'm not too late, am I? You've cured me.

DOCTOR PAYNE: As sure as eggs is eggs. But I need my papers back. I require my patients' charts.

SENATOR CATES: Submit to clinical trails. Work with me here. I can't fight alone on your behalf. Now let me look at that x-ray again. *(He holds it up to light. Sucks deeply on cigarette. Coughs)* Ahh. I feel better already. And so should you, Doc. So should you.

(Suddenly DOCTOR PAYNE *snatches X-ray from* SENATOR CATES, *and pops it in box. Something is obviously wrong.)*

SENATOR CATES: We'll stay in touch.

DOCTOR PAYNE: I'm sure we will.

*(*SENATOR CATES *exits.)*

DOCTOR PAYNE: Ruth. RUTH!!

RUTH: Yes, doctor.

DOCTOR PAYNE: *(Panicky)* Who's X-ray was that?

RUTH: That was yours. You know that. I told you, I spent all day at the Federal Building looking for the Senators X-ray, but couldn't find it. So I took one of yours. If you ask me they've misplaced it on purpose.

DOCTOR PAYNE: That was *my* X-ray?

RUTH: From last week. What's wrong, doctor? The pineal region is perfectly clear.

DOCTOR PAYNE: *(Panicked)* Yes. The pineal region is perfectly clear. But I'm not looking at the pineal region. Fuck!! I'm looking at this. Over here. By the cerebral hemispheres.

(Just then—from outside the window—an accident is heard.)

(First comes the prescient sound of brakes screeching, then the inevitable impact of collision.)

(RUTH runs to window to investigate. DOCTOR PAYNE keeps staring at X-rays.)

RUTH: Oh my God! It looks like the Senator.

(DOCTOR PAYNE crosses to look out window.)

DOCTOR PAYNE: Fuck! It is the Senator.

RUTH: He's not getting up.

(DOCTOR PAYNE then crosses back to stare at his X-rays.)

DOCTOR PAYNE: Can you fuckin believe this X-ray?!

RUTH: He's not getting up!

DOCTOR PAYNE: *(Pointing to x-ray)* That's a death sentence right there...

RUTH: And there's so much blood.

DOCTOR PAYNE: Right there in black and white.

(Lights fade...on everything except X-ray in box.

WHEN GOD SHEDS AN ACCIDENTAL TEAR

Scene 15

*(*DOCTOR PAYNE's *office. Later. He is haranguing* ROGER.
ROGER *is covered in blue paint.*

DOCTOR PAYNE: You stupid stupid fuck.

ROGER: I thought you'd be thankful.

DOCTOR PAYNE: For what?! For you being such a
stupid fuck!

ROGER: Don't talk to me like that.

DOCTOR PAYNE: Fuck you. You fuckin dickless
imbecile. That was the Senator you hit.

ROGER: It was an accident.

DOCTOR PAYNE: I thought you don't believe in
accidents.

ROGER: Not those I can't plan for.

DOCTOR PAYNE: He was on my team.

ROGER: He had government plates.

DOCTOR PAYNE: Yeah. Well, he's a senator. Not some
jerk from the Food and Drug Administration.

ROGER: You want I can still get that other bastard.
It's not too late you know...

DOCTOR PAYNE: Why don't you go somewhere and eat
your young. You incestuous motherfucker!

ROGER: Don't insult me.

DOCTOR PAYNE: You look like a fuckin giant tellytubby.

ROGER: Yeah, well I got a call back for the Blue Men audition. But they wanted me to shave my head and I said: "No way, God gave me my hair!"

DOCTOR PAYNE: *(Overlap)* Fuck! The Senator was gonna help me get approval. You understand what that means? You understand what you just did. The havoc you wrought?!

ROGER: I was only trying to help.

DOCTOR PAYNE: I didn't want your help.

ROGER: But you helped me...

DOCTOR PAYNE: I gave you a fuckin piece of toilet paper. And this is what I get in return?! Next time use your hand for Chrissake!

ROGER: But I thought you wanted this.

DOCTOR PAYNE: You thought wrong.

ROGER: You yourself said it was an *accident* there were not more *accidents* when you considered all the *accidents* waiting to happen. Or some shit like that.

DOCTOR PAYNE: That doesn't mean I wanted you to run anyone down. Especially not the Senator. He's not supposed to die like that. Not when he's got cancer. If and when he dies, he dies under *my* supervision, not some ill-conceived car collision.

ROGER: So I got the wrong guy. So what?! I was just pulling out of a parking spot when he happened to be crossing the street and the voice said: "Now. Floor it now!! Big fuckin deal. It's all part of the Lord Yahoo's plan anyway.

DOCTOR PAYNE: Get away from me. Get the fuck outta my sight.

ROGER: Like I said it's not too late to make amends. You want I can still fix...

DOCTOR PAYNE: Get out of my life before I call the cops.

ROGER: I wouldn't do that if I were you doc. Uh-uh, not that.

DOCTOR PAYNE: Fuckin psychotic hick.

(ROGER *picks up a scalpel and lunges at* DOCTOR PAYNE. *Threatening)*

ROGER: I asked you not to call me names. Even fuckin hicks like me can get sensitive. Now apologize.

DOCTOR PAYNE: Go on and kill me. I'm dying anyway you fuck.

ROGER: I don't care if you're dying or if you're already dead. You're still gonna apologize.

DOCTOR PAYNE: Fuck you you witless shit. You are responsible for the loss of millions of lives and you want me to say I'm sorry.

ROGER: Maybe God didn't want you to find a cure, Doc. Ever think of that? Maybe that was the plan all along.

DOCTOR PAYNE: My therapy could've saved millions and make my name immortal, but you fucked it all up.

ROGER: "And the *cancer* shall rule the earth and have dominion."

DOCTOR PAYNE: Now we're all doomed. How does that feel, huh? How does it feel to know you killed all these people?

ROGER: God does it every day, doc.

DOCTOR PAYNE: You stupid ignorant *blue* cunt!

ROGER: Sheds a fuckin tear like some monsoon over India and—poof! —ten thousand naked villagers are drowned in the blink of an eye.

DOCTOR PAYNE: I bet you don't even know where India is.

ROGER: So I guess to answer your question—I feel like God, Doctor. That's how I feel. And right now God wants an apology. From you.

(DOCTOR PAYNE *spits in* ROGER'*s face.*)

ROGER: You shouldn't have done that.

WHERE DESIRE ENDS AND THE PAIN OF LONELINESS BEGINS

Scene 16

(THERAPIST'*s office.* DOCTOR PAYNE *enters. He's late. On his head is his wife's wig.*

THERAPIST: You missed our last appointment.

DOCTOR PAYNE: Emergency at the clinic.

THERAPIST: You never called to explain.

DOCTOR PAYNE: I'm afraid I was the emergency.

THERAPIST: I'm sorry.

DOCTOR PAYNE: Had a lunatic patient/visitor who got slightly violent and had to be subdued.

THERAPIST: All better I hope.

DOCTOR PAYNE: On the contrary.

THERAPIST: Would you like to talk about it?

(DOCTOR PAYNE *shrugs.*)

THERAPIST: Something to do with the wig on your head...?

DOCTOR PAYNE: Oh this. It's my wife's.

THERAPIST: I thought she was—

DOCTOR PAYNE: She is. This was her wig when she lost her hair. From chemo. (*Lifts wig. We see he's bald.*)

THERAPIST: Are you—

DOCTOR PAYNE: Inoperable Glioblastoma Multiforme.

THERAPIST: How long have you known?

(DOCTOR PAYNE *shows* THERAPIST *X-ray*.)

DOCTOR PAYNE: I'd say I've got two, three months on the outside.

THERAPIST: Maybe you should get a second opinion.

DOCTOR PAYNE: Don't need to. I read X-rays like other people read the morning paper. And believe me that's no coffee stain in the corner.

THERAPIST: Did you just find out?

DOCTOR PAYNE: That's why I missed our last appointment. Didn't call. *(Pause)* Almost over-determined, wouldn't you say? "Experimental cancer doctor contracts cancer." *(Beat)* Some would call it divine justice.

THERAPIST: I'm sorry.

DOCTOR PAYNE: *(Shrugs)* I don't want my patients to know. Not yet. That's why I'm wearing the wig. But you are safe. You, my rented friend, are my little Swiss bank account full of ripe, juicy confidences. Tell me something: Will you really miss me once I'm gone?

THERAPIST: You still haven't answered my question.

DOCTOR PAYNE: What's that?

THERAPIST: When did you find out?

DOCTOR PAYNE: By accident. When I mixed up a pair of x-rays, I saw it by accident. I guess you can say that now the accident continues.

THERAPIST: Are you doing anything...?

DOCTOR PAYNE: Stopped masturbating, if that's what you mean. Gone cold jerky. Don't ask me to explain it, but somehow masturbating lost its appeal. Leaving my sticky genetic stain on some crumpled piece of Kleenex. *(He blows his nose.)* Pretty weird, don't you think...? Soon as I find out I'm mortal, I loose all interest in masturbating... *(Beat)* Hey, think that maybe if I found it again, rediscovered this...this *desire* to jerk off I could live longer. Would do you think...?

THERAPIST: I meant *therapy*-wise. What were you doing with treatment?

DOCTOR PAYNE: Treatment?

THERAPIST: What kind of treatment are you undergoing?

DOCTOR PAYNE: Don't really know yet. Right now I'm trying chemo so they can operate with a chance for a clear margin.

THERAPIST: What about your own technique?

DOCTOR PAYNE: What about it?

THERAPIST: Don't you see...this is a chance to finally test your own therapy, Doctor. *Without* F D A interference.

DOCTOR PAYNE: I said I don't know.

THERAPIST: You can do whatever you want. No outside intervention whatsoever...

DOCTOR PAYNE: Don't guilt me.

THERAPIST: But—

DOCTOR PAYNE: Can't you see I'm sacred? Too scared to even gamble or speculate anymore. Already I've drank my own piss like a fish with enlarged gills. Withstood enough chemo to kill a dozen wild horses. And I'm still afraid. But death is even stronger than my fear.

THERAPIST: What about your dreams...any dreams during this period? Perhaps we can find some comfort there.

DOCTOR PAYNE: Yes. Yes. I was naked. Lab coat at my feet. Standing entirely naked when the dead came to visit me and pay their respects. I asked them what it's like over there on the other side. I asked them to comfort me and deliver me from my fear. I even asked for a modicum of forgiveness.

THERAPIST: Did they answer...?

DOCTOR PAYNE: They told me they were thirsty. Very very thirsty. And if I could carry a glass of water to the other side, *one glass*, all would be forgiven. But apparently there's an enormous tax on importing things from one world to the next—much more than I could afford...so they asked if I would at least indulge them by spitting in their mouths. Sure, I said, I know how to do that. Just open wide.

(DOCTOR PAYNE *spits. But coughs up blood.* THERAPIST *is flustered, not knowing what to do, hands him a box of Kleenex*)

THERAPIST: Are you okay?

DOCTOR PAYNE: I'm fine except that suddenly everything feels so...far away, so temporary. Sitting in a chair that someone else sat in before. Breathing in air exhaled by someone else. Already I have begun mourning for myself, experiencing a bittersweet nostalgia for my own body. Lamenting the loss of arms and legs that will no longer transport me. Eyes that will no longer see the world for me. My ears, my tongue. A resumé of all the faculties that will abandon me soon as I die—and make me so fuckin lonely while I'm still alive.

(DOCTOR PAYNE *rises abruptly. Crosses to door*)

THERAPIST: Where are you going?

DOCTOR PAYNE: I just realized something. I need to live. Whatever that means, I need to live while I can.

THERAPIST: We still have ten minutes.

DOCTOR PAYNE: Exactly. And if I stay here they'll just turn into words.

THERAPIST: Wait.

(DOCTOR PAYNE *at door. Turns*)

THERAPIST: Your wig... It's on backwards.

(DOCTOR PAYNE *readjusts it.*)

DOCTOR PAYNE: Thanks. *(He exits.)*

(Lights fade.)

DOCTOR PAYNE DISCOVERS THAT THE BIRTH OF IRONY IS ALWAYS TRAGIC

Scene 17

(DOCTOR PAYNE's *office. Instead of art work the walls are now lined with slot machines. His arm hooked up to an intravenous, the balding doctor moves from one slot machine to the next. Slotting quarters and pulling the mechanical arm as he goes.)*

(DON *from F D A stands by the door, holding a heavy box.)*

DON: I've brought back some of your files.

DOCTOR PAYNE: Don't bother.

DON: The rest will be here by evening.

DOCTOR PAYNE: I said you needn't bother. Just throw them out.

DON: Sorry. But we're not authorized to do that.

DOCTOR PAYNE: Then put them next to the trash.
I'll write a note for the janitor.

DON: I thought this would make you happy.

DOCTOR PAYNE: Look. The only time I ever felt happy
was when I was holding my own pecker in my hands
or throwing my cards on the table...

DON: But the court ruled in your favor. Although we
are planning to appeal, just so you know. And next
time we'll be more careful with getting the proper
warrants.

DOCTOR PAYNE: There won't be a next time.

DON: What makes you say that?

(DOCTOR PAYNE *shrugs and pulls arm on slot machine.*)

DOCTOR PAYNE: Got change for a dollar...?

DON: Let me check. *(Digs in pockets)* What happened
to all your art work.

DOCTOR PAYNE: Vanished, like my hair.

DON: You sell it?

DOCTOR PAYNE: Traded it for these slot machines.

DON: But I thought—

DOCTOR PAYNE: I know, I know. Not the best deal in
the world, but who has time to haggle.

DON: But you said those paintings were priceless.

DOCTOR PAYNE: I did...? What can I say. Got tired of
looking at the same canvas every day...with the same
shapes and colors. Wanted something a little more
concrete, real, especially now that I'm about to become
a modern *abstraction* myself. *(Pulling slot)* These
machines are fully loaded with change you know.
That's what made it so expensive, so attractive...
that I might actually *win* something.

DON: Well, just in case you're interested, here's the Senator's file. We finally managed to locate it.

DOCTOR PAYNE: I'm sure you did. Now that he's...dead.

DON: We weren't concealing it.

DOCTOR PAYNE: But now you find it. How ironic.

DON: Not more than the Senator who came here to receive a clean bill of health, only to get killed on the way out.

DOCTOR PAYNE: That's the thing about irony, it's so *fuckin* ironic.

DON: I guess it is, yes.

DOCTOR PAYNE: Ironic and impersonal. Like an old fashioned accident. Because if you think about it, it could've been anyone. *(Insinuating to* DON*)* Anyone at all to get hit by that car. *(Pulls lever, waits.)* Ooo. Almost. Any more quarters?

DON: You're not looking too good.

DOCTOR PAYNE: Didn't know you cared. *(Puts the wig on)* This better?

*(*DON *hands* DOCTOR PAYNE *a pocketful of quarters.)*

DON: Here.

DOCTOR PAYNE: I'll pay you back with my winnings.

DON: Forget it.

*(*DOCTOR PAYNE *slots more quarters in the various machines.)*

DOCTOR PAYNE: So this man stumbles into a doctor's office and collapses with pain... *(Tell me if you've already heard this, I hate repeating old jokes.)* So the doctor asks the man what's the matter...what exactly hurts?
—"I have this terrible pain in my head, doctor, right behind my eyes", says the man.

—"Have you had it before?" Asks the doctor.
—"Yes. Come to think of it I have."
—"Well, now you have it again", says the doctor and
breaks down laughing.
   Hahaha...you like that? Hahaha. When I was a boy,
my father used to console me with that joke instead of
taking me to the doctor. That was his idea of empathy.
And saving money. Years later, before he died, I went
to visit him in the hospital. Poor guy was so afraid of
death you could see the sheet twitching over his body
like some small quiet avalanche. So I said: "Dad," I said,
"have

you ever experienced this kind of fear before?"
   —(See, I was already a doctor by then, so I had
authority now)— and he said, Yes... All his life he'd
been afraid of death. It terrified him all his life. And
so I said bending over him in my white lab coat, I said,
"Well then, now you have it again, except this time it's
gonna come true, your life is going to turn into death
and there's nothing I can do to help you." Then I
walked out the door and left him there. Crying. *(Slots
another quarter)* Most people, you have to realize,
confront death by choosing to avoid it. But not me. I
refuse to anesthetize myself with mindless distractions
and abstractions. For a while I actually thought the
urgency of my work would make death more
palatable—*my work and my impeccable art collection*—but
when you're dying it all seems so stupid and irrelevant.
(He frantically pulls the arm on several more slots.)

*(The machine lines up three of a kind. A cascade of quarters
come gushing out.)*

DOCTOR PAYNE: I've won!!! I win! I am finally winning!!

*(Just then DOCTOR PAYNE collapses to floor. Quarters
continue raining on his head.)*

DON: Doctor... Doctor! Are you alright. Help. Somebody help!

(RUTH runs in.)

RUTH: What did you do to him?

DON: He just collapsed.

RUTH: We need an ambulance. Call an ambulance.

(RUTH begins to give DOCTOR PAYNE mouth-to mouth. DON watches with a lagging twinge of jealously.)

RUTH: What are you waiting for? Call the ambulance.

DON: Is he dead?

RUTH: If he is, it's all your fuckin fault!

(Lights fade.)

THE CONTRITE DOCTOR PAYNE BEGS REDEMPTION AND OFFERS REPARATIONS IN A UNIVERSE THAT NO LONGER GIVES A SHIT

Scene 18

(Hospital room. DOCTOR PAYNE is lying in bed, semi-conscious. A NURSE [who was the MOTHER in earlier scenes] tends to him. This patent doubling is part of the theater.)

(Outside a fierce storm is wired with lightning and thunder.)

DOCTOR PAYNE: Ruth...

NURSE/MOTHER: She'll be back in a minute.

DOCTOR PAYNE: Am I in the hospital? Where am I?

NURSE/MOTHER: Can't you tell?

DOCTOR PAYNE: Is this pre-op or post-op?

NURSE/MOTHER: Soon these distinctions won't matter. Pre-op, post-op, I C U, D O A... it'll all be the same. Patient and doctor will be one.

DOCTOR PAYNE: Who are you?

NURSE/MOTHER: I am your nurse. Your nu*rrr*se. And in some cultures, Doctor, they keep the dead and the living in the same house for a whole week... together.

DOCTOR PAYNE: Am I dead then, is that it?

NURSE/MOTHER: Helps the living get used to their beloved's new silence. Like oil and vinegar, they mix the two together, the living and the dead...

DOCTOR PAYNE: You remind me of... someone.

NURSE/MOTHER: (*More to herself*) ...Trouble is, I sometimes forget which is which.

DOCTOR PAYNE: Where's Ruth?

NURSE/MOTHER: Out parking the car, poor woman, look at that rain.

DOCTOR PAYNE: Ruth!

NURSE/MOTHER: Wouldn't want to get a ticket and have your car booted while you're resting here at Intensive Care.

DOCTOR PAYNE: RUTH!

NURSE/MOTHER: Shh! I'm trying to get you all cleaned up before your guests arrive.

DOCTOR PAYNE: Guests...?

NURSE/MOTHER: You sound surprised.

DOCTOR PAYNE: Who would come visit me?

NURSE/MOTHER: Me...for one.

DOCTOR PAYNE: You...?

(NURSE/MOTHER *removes glasses, adopts a sudden Russian accent.*)

NURSE/MOTHER: Remember me now? Who do I remind you of now?

BOY/YURI: *(Offstage)* Mommy, mommy. I'm waiting for you.

MOTHER: Hear that? That's my boy. Made him wait on the balcony, because I didn't want him breathing in the hospital air. Lot's of germs here. But he wanted to see you.

(We hear the YURI singing offstage.)

MOTHER: Said he wants to serenade you one last time.

DOCTOR PAYNE: But I don't want to see anyone.

MOTHER: And the Senator is here too. There's a very long and distinguished line of people waiting for you. All your patients, now dead, waiting with outstretched arms...to meet you.

(In a hallucinatory state, enhanced by lightning and thunder and rain, DOCTOR PAYNE hears a menagerie of voices and sees a blend of shadows bouncing about the walls and in his head. Unearthing its own dramaturgy of death...)

("Let us in" "We want to see the Doctor." " Doctor! I need a doctor!!" etc.)

(Gradually some of the voices materialize in the room, overlapping, fast.)

SENATOR CATES: *(Enters)* Fucker had me run down. *(Spits)*

MOTHER: What about me? What he made me do to him.

DON: The runaround I had to go through. Do I look like an idiot?

ROGER: You're a very popular man, doc. Must put on quite a show.

YURI: He poisoned me with his medicine.

THERAPIST: Stop whining, all of you! You think you had it bad. I was his therapist. You know what that means? To visit the Petri dish of his diseased mind on a weekly basis. To try and understand something like...*this*!

(DOCTOR PAYNE *struggles out of bed and collapses.*)

DOCTOR PAYNE: *Go home! All of you. Get outta here! Leave me alone!!*

THERAPIST: Your hand, Doctor.

DOCTOR PAYNE: NO!!

THERAPIST: It's not a request, doctor. You of all people should know, death is rhetorical in its requests.

DOCTOR PAYNE: But I can't go, not yet. I'm on the verge of my great discovery.

THERAPIST: Oh that's right. The great genius here is about to cure cancer.

DOCTOR PAYNE: I want my coat.

(*Laughter all around. A general outcry from his "visitors": Cure me. /No, me first!/ What about me? /You promised me!!*)

DOCTOR PAYNE: I need my coat. Where's my white lab coat?

THERAPIST: Look around you doc. It's too late for a cure. You of all people should know that. There is no cure for life. Your hand!

DOCTOR PAYNE: No. No...

(DOCTOR PAYNE *tries to crawl away but they block him, converging.*)

THERAPIST: Are you afraid? Don't be afraid. Your wife is already waiting for you.

DOCTOR PAYNE: *(Panicked)* My wife...?

(RUTH enters with wig on. Full nagging force.)

RUTH/WIFE: *(Accent)* Are you ready, dear?

DOCTOR PAYNE: NO! *(He cowers under the blanket.)*

RUTH/WIFE: Did you turn down the heat like I asked you to?

DOCTOR PAYNE: I'm sorry, hon, I'm sorry.

RUTH/WIFE: And what about that shirt, you want to wear that shirt, just make sure I'm not in the same room, on the same day.

DOCTOR PAYNE: *(Resisting)* Why can't you just leave me alone. All of you. Please!

(Panicked, the Doctor disappears under the blanket.)

RUTH: *(Sheds the wig)* Hey, doc. Doc. It's me Ruth. Don't you recognize me?

DOCTOR PAYNE: Ruth! RUTH!! Thank god it's you. I thought— Help me. RUTH!! Help me.

(DOCTOR PAYNE hugs RUTH desperately.)

RUTH: It's alright Doctor. Everything will be alright.

DOCTOR PAYNE: Am I dead, Ruth? Am I already dead?

RUTH: Shhh! You should be in bed.

DOCTOR PAYNE: *(Peeking from under blanket)* Are they still here?

RUTH: A little more pain killer and you'll be just fine.

DOCTOR PAYNE: No. No pain killer. The curtains. Just open the curtains. I need light.

RUTH: But it's dark outside. *(She parts the curtains.)*
See...? Except for a little flash of lightning it's all dark
and wet out there. Had a terrible time parking the car.

DOCTOR PAYNE: *(Overlap)* I don't care. I don't care
All this time, cancer's been spreading its thick branches
throughout my body, drowning me in darkness.
Where is the light when you need it, Ruth? More than
air I need light.

(Lightning flashes in the sky, briefly lighting up the room.
DOCTOR PAYNE *breathes in the light.)*

DOCTOR PAYNE: What are you doing, Ruth? I thought
I said no pain killer.

RUTH: It's for your own good, Doc.

DOCTOR PAYNE: I want to *experience* my death.

RUTH: Who said anything about dying? We're here
to help you get rid of the poison inside you.

ROGER: Like cutting the back of your own hair.

SENATOR CATES: We're going to help find the cancer.
And then banish it.

MOTHER: All of us.

YURI: We want to play doctor too.

DOCTOR PAYNE: Make them go away, Ruth. Please.

(They wheel up a hospital screen. Only his head remains
visible. Various surgical implements are set up for a
vivisection.)

DOCTOR PAYNE: Ruth. What are they doing to me?

RUTH: I told you to take more pain killer.

(They amputate his arms.)

DON: We're going after the cancer, doc. Carve out
a little of God's clean margin here.

SENATOR CATES: *Clean* like an angels' underwear.

ROGER: I'm not sure he believes in God.

THERAPIST: Time like this, it hardly matters what he believes in. It's the *sacrifice* itself that counts. Kidney or penis? If you had to choose, which would it be. Penis or kidney?

ROGER: That's too easy.

DON: We're just warming up here.

DOCTOR PAYNE: I don't know.

MOTHER: Important to make choice.

ROGER: If we can find just one clean and righteous organ in this Sodom and Gomorrah you call your body, maybe you will be saved.

RUTH: I got it I got it! *(She removes a kidney.)* Who wants a kidney?

SENATOR CATES: Are you kidding? Look at that thing. It's diseased.

YURI: It smells Ma, it really stinks bad.

MOTHER: Breathe through your mouth.

THERAPIST: My God. How could you live with yourself?! It's so putrid.

YURI: Gross!

DON: Couldn't even donate this to science.

RUTH: Keep looking everyone. The goodness must be there somewhere. I know it must.

DON: O K. This one's a little harder. Liver or penis.

DOCTOR PAYNE: I need my liver....

MOTHER: It's your choice. Penis or liver?

DON: Don't worry, doc. We're not just going to burn you like a witch. No. We're planning to examine the evidence carefully. Clinically. Seek some kind of forensic atonement.

RUTH: Who wants a liver?

(They pass his organ around like a hot potato.)

THERAPIST: You're even uglier on the inside than out.

SENATOR CATES: Cut to the chase already. Heart or penis. What's it gonna be?

DOCTOR PAYNE: What's going on Ruth?

MOTHER: Penis or heart?

DON: Now that's always a tough one. Seeing as how they're so connected.

DOCTOR PAYNE: Make them stop, Ruth. Please.

RUTH: It'll be over soon.

MOTHER: Penis or heart? Make your choice before it spreads.

DOCTOR PAYNE: I can't answer that...

MOTHER: Sure you can.

RUTH: Doctor!

(They all jump back in awe. Staring at DOCTOR PAYNE's *loins.)*

DOCTOR PAYNE: What? What is it...?!

RUTH: My God!

MOTHER: Is that your answer?

SENATOR CATES: Have you name shame at last, son?

MOTHER: Cover your eyes Yuri.

ROGER: Saving the best for last, eh.

THERAPIST: How can you at a time like this.

(DOCTOR PAYNE, *along with everyone else, looks down to admire his relentless, unapologetic erection.*)

DOCTOR PAYNE: I'm sorry. Must've been that night sky outside working its secret charms on me. The slow-migrating clouds drifting like giant metastasized tumors. Isn't it beautiful? Romantic? Doesn't the broad night sky remind you of a beautiful giant X-ray? Like it was God's very own lungs exposed up there in the smoky night air.

DON: *(Re penis)* It's got something written on it.

SENATOR CATES: I think it's German.

ROGER: Mine's in English.

THERAPIST: What doesn't kill me only makes me stronger.

DOCTOR PAYNE: *(Like Samson)* GOD!!! Feels like I have the erection of a hanged man. Will someone not help release this pressure...?!

(*Armless, he turns to his respective guests, his proud erection begging to be appeased.*)

RUTH: Looks hard enough to break bricks with.

THERAPIST: Nobody touch that.

SENATOR CATES: Wouldn't dream of it.

DOCTOR PAYNE: I beg you please.

MOTHER: Not even to save my boy's life.

DOCTOR PAYNE: How about you Roger. Please.

ROGER: All of a sudden he remembers my name. Needs my help.

DOCTOR PAYNE: Release me Senator.

SENATOR CATES: First dink my piss, hahahaha.

DOCTOR PAYNE: Please, someone, Ruth... Just one last time. Touch it lightly like a bee pollinating a flower. I beg you. The pain of this unmet desire is killing me. Will nobody help me?

(RUTH *moves to touch.*)

THERAPIST: Nobody touch his cursed happiness! If that is his only true goodness let it stay that way.

(Another injection of lightning, crash of thunder.)

DOCTOR PAYNE: How about you Ruth. Haven't I been good to you...?

RUTH: I'm sorry doctor. They're all waiting.

DOCTOR PAYNE: Fine, go! All of you. What the fuck do I care? I have my erection to keep me company! Just one small request, Ruth. Wheel me closer to the window, before you go. *(Lightning)* So I can look one last time at God's x-ray lighting up the sky. Filling the room with its unbearable beauty. You see, I'm not embarrassed to stare back at beauty. And I will cherish this last moment as only the dying can cherish it. Every last thing a sudden souvenir of something not yet gone. But already leaving. The last smile and the last goodbye.

RUTH: Goodybe Doctor.

DOCTOR PAYNE: Goodbye Ruth, Goodbye.

(RUTH *wheels* DOCTOR PAYNE *to window and exits. Against the hospital screen, the magnified shadow of his penis is intermittently made visible by lightning. Rapture reads on his face. Increasing with each stroke of lightning.)*

DOCTOR PAYNE: Like the blind and neutered Samson, your favorite atheist pleads with you one last time God. Deliver me from my self. That is the steepled prayer of Mind over Matter. Art over Life. Christ you've got a beautiful set of lungs Lord! Anyone ever tell you that? Your x-ray lighting up the room... like some mysterious stained glass window to the soul. This must be what the prophets call an epiphany, if I ever saw one. And so if I must be punished, let it be with pleasure.

(More lightning. Thunder competing. DOCTOR PAYNE's *excitement rising in pitch.)*

DOCTOR PAYNE: Oh yes, oh yes, oh god. No hands. Only this, my thought. Pure passion...unfettered desire. YES! YYESSSS!!!! *(He comes and collapses. Pause. He looks up.)* Okay Death, come and get me while I'm hot! Strike the lightning rod of my soul. Because you couldn't be catching me at a better time. No, no better time than this.

(Lightning enters through hospital window and strikes the silhouetted tip of DOCTOR PAYNE's *penis. He expires.)*

END OF PLAY

www.ingramcontent.com/pod-product-compliance
Lightning Source LLC
Chambersburg PA
CBHW052156090426
42741CB00010B/2300